DELHI

DELHI

Delhi has a reputation of being a noisy, chaotic, and somewhat unruly city, and there is some truth to this stereotype. Indeed, Delhi has all the bustle of a capital city with the added chaos of India thrown in for good measure. The city has a population of more than 16 million, and the streets and markets are almost always at least somewhat crowded. It's also loud: really loud. Delhi's drivers love honking their horns (you'll find this in other parts of India too), and this is generally not out of aggression so much as the inevitable boredom that arises in the city's incessant traffic jams. However, it's also a beautiful green city filled with stately tree-lined boulevards, quiet parks, trendy cafés, and some of the most incredible archaeological sites in the world. In fact, you'll find that the travelers who complain the most about India's capital have often seen very little of the city beyond the admittedly hectic Old Delhi and the grimy backpacker enclave of Paharganj.

Delhi is also the most culturally rich city in the country and is home to a great number of cultural centers, art galleries, media outfits, publishers, and top-notch educational institutes. On any given evening, you'll have a great number of activities and events to choose from, and you'll never go hungry in this city of foodies—Delhi has an amazing culinary scene. The shopping is fantastic and generally quite affordable, and the nightlife is getting better by the day. Most of all, Delhi has an incredible

HIGHLIGHTS

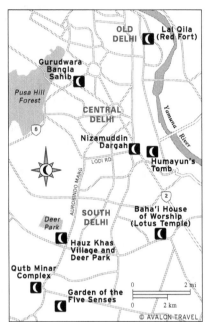

◖ Lal Qila (Red Fort): At the heart of Old Delhi, this enormous 17th-century fort was once the seat of the Mughal Empire (page 10).

◖ Gurudwara Bangla Sahib: Behold the beauty of this historic Sikh *gurudwara* (page 14).

◖ Nizamuddin Dargah: This shrine of Sufi saint Nizamudin Auliya gets particularly animated on Thursday evenings, when traditional Qawwali performances are staged (page 18).

◖ Humayun's Tomb: The tomb of Humayun, the second Mughal emperor, exemplifies early Muhgal architectural aesthetics (page 19).

◖ Baha'i House of Worship (Lotus Temple): This serene lotus-shaped temple is for adherents of the Baha'i faith or anyone seeking solace (page 21).

◖ Garden of the Five Senses: An enchanting garden specially designed to stimulate the five senses, adorned with statues, installations, and plants (page 23).

◖ Hauz Khas Village and Deer Park: Bourgeois bohemia prevails at this charming South Delhi arts and fashion village (page 23).

◖ Qutb Minar Complex: This amazing collection of towers, tombs, and architectural oddities is one of the oldest archaeological sites in Delhi (page 24).

LOOK FOR ◖ TO FIND RECOMMENDED SIGHTS, ACTIVITIES, DINING, AND LODGING.

selection of important historical sights and tourist attractions, and the government has gone to great lengths to keep the city's cultural heritage well preserved, even as the great capital city becomes increasingly globalized.

HISTORY

Archaeologists believe that Delhi has been inhabited for at least three millennia. It is thought to be the location of Indraprastha, a city mentioned in the ancient text the *Mahabharata* as the capital of the Pandava people, as evidenced by excavation work done at Central Delhi's Purana Qila, the likely site of the ancient city. Delhi city was officially founded in 736, when Anangpal of the Tomar clan, who claimed to be descendants of the Pandavas, set up a city called Lal Kot at the present-day Qutb Minar complex. By the end of the 12th century, the city was taken over by Prithviraj III of the short-lived Chauhan Dynasty, and then taken over by Muhammad of Ghor, who ruled until his death in 1206. For the next 320 years, Delhi was ruled by a succession of Turkic clans before finally succumbing to Babur, the founder of the Mughal Empire, at the First Battle of Panipat in 1526.

Delhi remained under Mughal rule well into the 19th century, with the exception of a few years when it was taken over from Babur's son Humayun by Sher Shah Suri, founder of the short-lived Sur Dynasty; Humayun later regained control over Delhi in 1555, only to die the next year. In the mid-18th century, the Maratha rulers from the south took control of Delhi, indirectly ruling its people via the de facto Mughal emperor. However, in 1803 the British East India Company defeated the Marathas at the Battle of Delhi of the Second Anglo-Maratha War, effectively taking over Delhi's indirect rule. A Mughal emperor remained on the throne until the 1857 Indian Rebellion (a.k.a. the Sepoy Mutiny), during which the East India Company exiled the last Mughal emperor (Bahadur Shah II) to Rangoon and transferred its power to the British crown. Calcutta was declared India's capital, which it remained until 1911, when King George V of England, emperor of British India, declared that Delhi would once again be capital. He commissioned architect Edwin Lutyens to design the city of New Delhi, and the part of Central Delhi characterized by its well-planned leafy avenues is known as Lutyens' Delhi to this day.

The 20th century was one of great change for the capital. After Independence, India was divided from Pakistan and what is now Bangladesh. The states of Punjab and Bengal were split in half along the Radcliffe Line, a culturally arbitrary yet incredibly significant border named for the British lawyer who had never been to India yet was charged with chalking out the Republic's new frontiers in all of five weeks. This division, known as Partition, led to a great number of Hindu and Sikh Punjabis fleeing Pakistan, and many Muslim Punjabis escaping west to Pakistan. Millions of people were displaced during this time, many having to flee their homes overnight. Those who didn't die en route had to start over with nothing in their new homes. Many of them headed to what was then known as Western Pakistan ended up settling in Lahore; those coming into India came in great numbers to Delhi, and much of South Delhi was built up as a result of this mass immigration. Delhi consequently has a huge Punjabi population (as well as a sizeable number of Bengali people, most of whom live in the leafy Chittaranjan Park neighborhood, not far from the landmark Lotus Temple). As the capital, the city has also seen waves of immigration from around the country, and pretty much every community in India is represented. In the 1960s, many Tibetans fled the Chinese occupation of their homeland and settled in India, and these days the capital is home to a sizable number of second- and third-generation Tibetans. India's economic boom over the past couple of decades has also led to an influx of expatriates, and it's no longer uncommon to meet people from around the world who have made this diverse city their adopted home.

PLANNING YOUR TIME

It's unfortunate that so many people see Delhi as simply a stopping-off point for exploring other destinations, especially considering how rich the city is in history and culture. If you have the time, you should attempt to spend at least three or four days here, and while realistically this isn't enough time to visit all of Delhi's sights, it's enough time to visit a handful and take advantage of the city's exceptional shopping. You can easily spend a full day in Old Delhi alone, and as it's arguably the most chaotic part of town, you may want to do it all at once. You can cover Central Delhi's main attractions on your second day, and save a third day for South Delhi and a bit of shopping. Just one thing to keep in mind when planning your itinerary: Delhi's traffic is notoriously bad, so leave plenty of time in your schedule for delays, and try to avoid traveling at peak rush hour times.

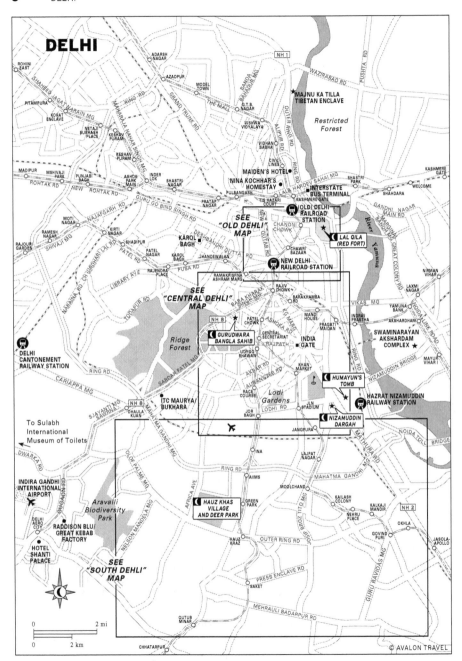

DELHI

© AVALON TRAVEL

Central Delhi is arguably the most convenient spot to stay in town due to its proximity to many major sights. This part of town also has the best access to the Metro, as it's where many of the major lines converge. However, many visitors prefer the calm of South Delhi, where many of the city's most charming independent hotels are located. Some people prefer the rustic feel of staying in Old Delhi, but there's not much in terms of restaurants, and the shopping options are more geared toward local residents.

SAFETY AND SCAMS

Contrary to popular belief, Delhi is actually a very safe city for foreign visitors. Your main concerns are likely to be related to health. It's not unheard of for visitors, especially those who are gung-ho about eating street food, to succumb to the notorious "Delhi belly." The air quality here is also not great (although it has improved dramatically over the past decade), and asthma sufferers may have trouble breathing.

Like any large capital city, there's plenty of crime in Delhi. However, violent crime directed at foreigners is rare. That said, it's still a good idea to be vigilant of your surroundings and your belongings. Sexual harassment and groping are fairly common—if anybody touches you in a way that makes you feel uncomfortable, tell them to stop immediately, and don't smile while doing it. If someone gropes you, feel free to slap him. In crowded areas, meaning most of Delhi, keep track of your wallet, camera, and phone at all times, and don't keep any valuables within easy reach of potential thieves.

There are a few common scams to be aware of. The most common is fake international tourist bureaus. Here's how it works: You're at New Delhi Railway Station about to board a train. A man approaches you and says he's an Indian Railways employee and asks to see your ticket. When you show him your ticket, he claims it's either fake or invalid and you will need to buy a new one from the international ticketing counter. He will then lead you out of the train station and across the street to a travel agent with a sign claiming that they are the "official international tourist bureau." The only international tourist ticketing office in all of Delhi is *inside* the New Delhi Railway Station on the first floor, near the Paharganj entrance. Also note that the only people you need to show your ticket to are uniformed police officers who sometimes screen baggage at the station entrance, and uniformed trainmasters.

The most frightening scam in Delhi takes place primarily in Paharganj and involves hypnosis, coercion, and mind control. You may be approached by a turbaned man who will want to demonstrate his psychic powers to you. He'll show you an old class photo and ask you to choose one person from it and concentrate on that person. Then he'll tell you, correctly, who you were thinking of. Next, he'll guess your favorite color, details about your father, and all kinds of other strange things. After that, he'll invite you to tea, and soon you'll find yourself walking to the ATM and pulling out a large donation for him. It's difficult to say how this scam works, but while I've personally never fallen for it, I have seen plenty of foreigners marching trancelike to a Paharganj ATM with one of these tricksters in tow.

Most scams in Delhi involve overcharging for services. Budget guesthouses may tack on breakfasts that were never ordered or fees that were never disclosed—this rarely happens at nicer places. Another scam often spoken about and rarely witnessed is the old poo-on-the-shoe trick. You'll be walking along when suddenly a bit of animal dung splats squarely on your shoes. A shoeshine boy will run up and start scrubbing off the muck without even asking, and then demand an exorbitant price for the service.

ORIENTATION

Delhi is an enormous, sprawling city, and crossing from one end to the other can take hours.

The city is divided into Old Delhi, North Delhi, East Delhi, West Delhi, Central Delhi, and South Delhi. The suburban "satellite cities" of Gurgaon and Noida are also often considered part of greater Delhi (also known as the National Capital Region, or NCR), although both cities have their own administration. Fortunately, most of the sights are located in South, Central, and Old Delhi, and these are the three parts of town where visitors will spend most, if not all, of their time. These three areas also have the best food and accommodations options in town, and there's very little reason to stay elsewhere.

Old Delhi has the most Mughal-era sights and is more or less synonymous with Shahjahanabad, the 17th-century city built by Mughal emperor Shahjahan of Taj Mahal fame. This area is best known for its old houses and mosques, lively markets, and street food. It's also one of the louder and dirtier parts of town, and most visitors prefer to come for a day and then return to their hotels in Central or South Delhi.

Much of Central Delhi was designed under British rule by well-known architect Edwin Lutyens. This gives it a bit more of a colonial—and somewhat European—feel, and the area is characterized by long tree-flanked boulevards, regal government buildings and palaces, and chic shopping districts, such as Connaught Place and Khan Market. It's also home to a number of Lodi and Mughal-era tombs.

South Delhi is a bit more of a hodgepodge, with everything from modern temples to crumbling ruins. This part of town began to develop rapidly after Independence, and today it's one of the trendier parts of Delhi, especially among the middle and upper echelons of society. Here you'll find all the typical signs of globalization (McDonald's, shopping malls), as well as some of the best shopping and dining options in the city.

One of the best ways to get around Delhi is by Metro. This system of underground and aboveground train stations covers a good deal of the city, and it is expected to expand its reach considerably within the next 5-10 years. Currently only some sights, restaurants, and hotels are within walking distance of a Metro station. Listings without a corresponding station are too far to walk. That said, you can save a lot of money by taking the Metro to the nearest station and then catching an auto or cycle rickshaw to your destination.

Sights

Delhi has tons of sights, most of which are either religious or historical (although some, such as Old Delhi's Jama Masjid, are a combination of both). The most popular sight in Old Delhi is the Lal Qila, or Red Fort, which many people visit in the morning, seeing other nearby sights in the afternoon. Central Delhi has a wider variety of sights, ranging from landmarks such as India Gate to crumbling old tombs. It's also home to many of the city's best-known museums. South Delhi is home to many interesting religious sites, including the Kalkaji Mandir and the string of temples on Chhatarpur

Mandir Road. There are few major sights in North Delhi and East Delhi, save the Majnu Ka Tilla Tibetan enclave and the Swaminarayan Akshardham Complex, respectively.

OLD DELHI
◖ Lal Qila (Red Fort)

The Lal Qila (sunrise-sunset Tues.-Sun., Rs. 250 foreigners, Rs. 10 Indians, video Rs. 25; sound and light show Rs. 80 adults, Rs. 30 children), or Red Fort, was built by Emperor Shahjahan after he shifted his base from Agra to Delhi and established the city of

CAPITAL OF CULTURE

© MARGOT BIGG

The India Habitat Centre hosts cultural events almost every day.

Delhi is not only the capital of India but also the capital of the country's cultural life. Nowhere else in in the country will you find such a diverse array of regular cultural events and performances, and there are usually plenty of events to choose from every night of the week.

IF YOU WANT TO . . .

- **Catch a play:** Head to one of the many theaters in the Mandi House area of central Delhi, the capital's undisputed theater district.

- **Browse modern art:** A large number of the city's finest modern art galleries are clustered in South Delhi's Hauz Khas Village.

- **Take in a classical music recital:** Both the India Habitat Centre (IHC) and the India International Centre (IIC) have regular music performances and are within a few minutes of each other in the south-central Lodi Road area.

Shahjahanabad. Construction on this red sandstone citadel began on April 16, 1639, and the project was finished exactly nine years later on April 16, 1648. The massive octagonal fort sits on 50 hectares and is surrounded by 2.4 kilometers of walls as well as a moat that once connected to the Yamuna River. In other words, it's a huge place that merits at least a two-hour visit.

Entering through the **Lahore Gate,** you'll pass through the **Chhatta Chowk,** a roofed arcade full of two-story apartments that have been converted into shops. The next building is the Naubat Khana, a house of drums where music was once played five times a day. This three-story structure features carved designs that were once painted in gold.

The next building is the **Diwan-i-Aam** (Hall of Public Audiences), which was once decorated

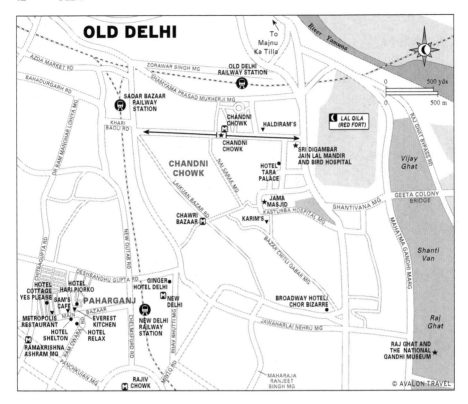

with gilded stucco. This was where both the emperor and the prime minister received the public (the prime minister even had his own marble dais to stand on, complete with inlaid precious stone). A series of panels on the back wall depicts flowers and birds in stone inlay, as well as Orpheus with his lute; they are believed to have been crafted by Florentine jeweler Austin de Bordeaux. These panels were transferred to the Victoria and Albert Museum in London but were returned in 1903 at the insistence of Lord Curzon, India's Viceroy at the time.

Facing the Yamuna River, on the south side of the fort's wall, the **Mumtaz Mahal** is believed to have been built by Shahjahan's queen, Arjumand Banu Begum. Today, it is a museum of Mughal history featuring art, armory,

manuscripts, and astronomy tools spread over six themed galleries. North of the museum are the **Rang Mahal** (Palace of Color) and the **Khas Mahal** (Private Palace). The former contains six apartments, including two Sheesh Mahal (Mirror Palace) rooms, which are decorated with small fragments of mirrors arranged to create a beautiful display at night with reflected candlelight. The Khas Mahal comprises three rooms used for praying, sleeping, and dressing.

The **Diwan-i-Khas** (Hall of Private Audiences) sits just beyond the Khas Mahal and features aisles of decorated arches and a wooden ceiling that was painted in 1911 and topped with *chhatris* (canopies) on each of its four corners. Just beyond the Diwan-i-Khas is the **Hammam,** or bathhouse, which features marble inlaid floors. There are three rooms, and the center room features a large basin. The western room, from where the heating was supplied, was where people would go to take hot steam baths, and the eastern room, used for changing, has three fountains that once spouted rose water. Just west of the Hammam is the small **Moti Masjid** (Pearl Mosque), which was used by Aurangzeb. Note the small black marble outlines of prayer rugs that decorate the walls of the prayer hall. On the roof of the structure are three domes that are believed to have formerly been plated with copper.

Sri Digambar Jain Lal Mandir and Bird Hospital

At the east end of Chandni Chowk, just a few paces from the Red Fort, is the red sandstone Sri Digambar Jain Lal Mandir and Bird Hospital (Chandni Chowk, Metro: Chandni Chowk, tel. 11/3290-9216, 10 A.M.-5 P.M. daily, free).

The Lal Mandir is dedicated to Parshvanath, the 23rd Tirthankara (enlightened ascetic) of the Jain faith, and was built in 1628, making it one of Delhi's oldest temples. The Lal Mandir is best known for its Bird Hospital, which has been treating sick and injured birds since 1956. The hospital admits upward of 60 birds a day, and contrary to popular belief, the strictly vegetarian Jain veterinarians and attendants here do not turn away birds of prey.

Jama Masjid

India's largest mosque, the Jama Masjid (between Chowri Bazaar Rd. and Meena Bazaar Rd., Metro: Chandni Chowk, 7 A.M.-noon and 1:30-6:30 P.M. daily, free, camera Rs. 200) was built by Shahjahan from 1650 to 1656 at a cost of around one million rupees. The red sandstone and white marble mosque was extensively used by the emperor and other royalty, and there's a terrace above the eastern gateway

© RAJAT DEEP RANA

Gurudwara Bangla Sahib is an important place of pilgrimage for Sikhs.

that was originally reserved primarily for the nobility. The two minarets here stand 40 meters tall and are worth a visit if you're not afraid of heights or stairs, but disappointingly, women are not allowed to visit them without a male companion. On the western side, a large prayer hall has a beautiful 11-arch facade and is capped with three black and striped marble domes. The main courtyard here is nearly 100 square meters and can accommodate up to 20,000 people.

Raj Ghat and the National Gandhi Museum

On the banks of the Yamuna River, Raj Ghat (MG Rd., sunrise-sunset daily, free) marks the spot where Mahatma Gandhi was cremated on January 31, 1948, the day after he was assassinated. A memorial in the form of a black marble platform has been placed here with "Hey Ram" (allegedly, though debatably, Gandhi's last words) written in Devanagari, the Hindi script, on its side. The memorial is regularly decorated with fresh flowers, and there's an eternal flame. The memorial itself is not much to see, and most visitors just stop by for a few minutes to pay their respects, but the surrounding grassy knolls are good for stroll.

Just across the main road from Raj Ghat is the National Gandhi Museum (opposite Raj Ghat, tel. 11/2331-1793, www.gandhimuseum. org, 10 A.M.-5 P.M. Tues.-Sun., free), which houses a large collection of art and artifacts related to Gandhi and the freedom movement, ranging from old documents to audiovisual recordings of the Mahatma. They also have a library and a small collection of books for sale, including some hard-to-find titles.

CENTRAL DELHI
Gandhi Smriti

The last home of Mahatma Gandhi, where he was assassinated on January 30, 1948, was turned into a museum in the 1980s and dubbed Gandhi Smriti (Birla House, 5 Tees January Lane, tel. 11/2301-2843, http://gandhismriti.gov. in, 10 A.M.-5 P.M. Tues.-Sun., free). The museum is filled with old photographs of the Mahatma as well as a few personal effects and lots of miniature scenes depicting various significant events in Gandhi's life. The museum is divided into three sections that deal with keeping Gandhi's memory alive, explaining his values, and illustrating the emphasis he placed on serving others.

◖ Gurudwara Bangla Sahib

Delhi's best-known *gurudwara* (Sikh place of worship), the Gurudwara Bangla Sahib (Ashok Rd., Metro: Patel Chowk, tel. 11/2336-5486, 24 hours daily, free) was originally a bungalow belonging to Raja Jai Singh of the Mughal Empire. Guru Har Krishan, the eighth guru of Sikhism, stayed here during a trip to Delhi in the 17th century. During his residency, the Guru helped smallpox victims from this house, although he later ended up dying of that disease. Raja Jai Singh then built a small tank over the bungalow's well, and these days, the devout come to take holy water, which is referred to as *amrit* (nectar) and is believed to have healing powers.

The bungalow was later transformed into a *gurudwara,* and today the complex also houses a school and a hospital as well as an art gallery devoted to spiritual and historical art and a library full of books on Sikh history and faith, both of which are open to visitors. As per Sikh tradition, the *gurudwara* also houses a volunteer-run *langar* (community kitchen) where people of all faiths and backgrounds are invited to eat communally for free (of course, those who can always donate or help out with food preparation and serving).

The massive white-marble *gurudwara* acts as a place of solace for both Sikh and non-Sikh visitors alike, and the mood feels calmer and more orderly than most other sights in Delhi. Adding to the ambience is the meditative chants from the Guru Granth Sahib, the Sikh holy book, which devotees read out melodically from the

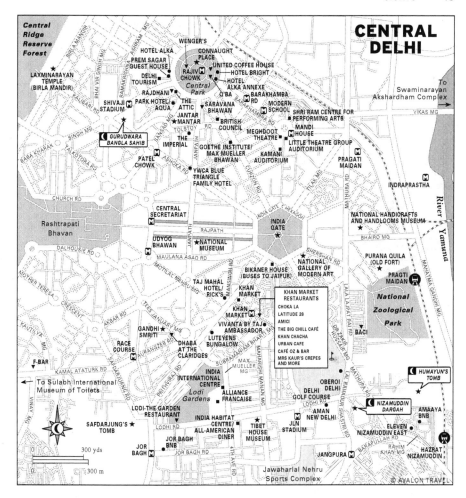

Central Delhi

Central Ridge Reserve Forest

LAXMINARAYAN TEMPLE (BIRLA MANDIR)

SHIVAJI STADIUM

WENGER'S
HOTEL ALKA
PREM SAGAR GUEST HOUSE
CONNAUGHT PLACE
UNITED COFFEE HOUSE
DELHI TOURISM
RAJIV CHOWK
HOTEL BRIGHT
HOTEL ALKA ANNEXE
RAJDHANI
PARK HOTEL
Central Park
Q'BA
BARAKHAMBA RD
MODERN SCHOOL
THE ATTIC
AQUA
SARAVANA BHAWAN
SHRI RAM CENTRE FOR PERFORMING ARTS
JANTAR MANTAR
BRITISH COUNCIL
MEGHDOOT THEATRE
MANDI HOUSE
TOLSTOY RD
GOETHE INSTITUTE/ MAX MUELLER BHAWAN
LITTLE THEATRE GROUP AUDITORIUM
GURUDWARA BANGLA SAHIB
THE IMPERIAL
KAMANI AUDITORIUM
PRAGATI MAIDAN
PATEL CHOWK
YWCA BLUE TRIANGLE FAMILY HOTEL
INDRAPRASTHA
VIKAS MG
To Swaminarayan Akshardham Complex

Rashtrapati Bhavan

CENTRAL SECRETARIAT
RAJPATH
UDYOG BHAWAN
NATIONAL MUSEUM
MAULANA ASAD RD
INDIA GATE
NATIONAL HANDICRAFTS AND HANDLOOMS MUSEUM
BHAIRO MG
PURANA QILA (OLD FORT)
PRAGTI MAIDAN
National Zoological Park
River Yamuna

BIKANER HOUSE (BUSES TO JAIPUR)
NATIONAL GALLERY OF MODERN ART
TAJ MAHAL HOTEL/ RICK'S
KHAN MARKET
KHAN MARKET
VIVANTA BY TAJ AMBASSADOR
LUTEYENS BUNGALOW
GANDHI SMRITI
RACE COURSE
DHABA AT THE CLARIDGES
F-BAR

KHAN MARKET RESTAURANTS
CHOKA LA
LATITUDE 28
AMICI
THE BIG CHILL CAFÉ
KHAN CHACHA
URBAN CAFE
CAFÉ OZ & BAR
MRS KAUR'S CREPES AND MORE

BACI

To Sulabh International Museum of Toilets
INDIA INTERNATIONAL CENTRE
Lodi Gardens
ALLIANCE FRANCAISE
OBEROI DELHI
DELHI GOLF COURSE
HUMAYUN'S TOMB
NIZAMUDDIN DARGAH
AMAAYA BNB

LODI-THE GARDEN RESTAURANT
INDIA HABITAT CENTRE/ ALL-AMERICAN DINER
TIBET HOUSE MUSEUM
AMAN NEW DELHI
JLN STADIUM
ELEVEN NIZAMUDDIN EAST

SAFDARJUNG'S TOMB
JOR BAGH BNB
JOR BAGH RD
JANGPURA
HAZRAT NIZAMUDDIN

Jawaharlal Nehru Sports Complex

300 yds
300 m

© AVALON TRAVEL

gurudwara's sanctum. Out of respect for the sanctity of the sight and Sikh tradition, men and women alike should remove their shoes and cover their heads before entering the complex.

India Gate

Although its real name is the "All India War Memorial Arch," everybody refers to this 42-meter-high freestanding arch simply as India Gate. The arch commemorates the service of the 90,000 Indian soldiers who lost their lives in World War I. The names of the 13,516 Indian and British soldiers who died fighting in the Third Anglo-Afghan War and on the treacherous Northwest Frontier (in present-day Pakistan) are engraved on the archway. There's also an ever-burning Amar Jawan Jyoti (Flame of the Eternal Soldier), which commemorates the tomb of the Unknown Soldier. Despite the fact that India Gate represents some rather somber events in history, it actually feels more like a party spot most of the time, especially in

© RAJAT DEEP RANA

Central Delhi's India Gate

four-in-one calculation tool that has a number of functions, including determining the entry of the sun into Cancer and finding meridians in four spots (two in Europe, one in Japan, and one in the Pacific Ocean). Unfortunately, the instruments fall in the shadow of the tall buildings of nearby Connaught Place and are thus of little astronomical use today. There's also a small temple dedicated to the god Bhairava on the site, which is also believed to have been built by Sawai Jai Singh II.

Laxminarayan Temple (Birla Mandir)

One of the many temples built by the Birla family of industrialists, the Laxminarayan Temple (near Gole Market, Mandir Marg, Metro: Ramakrishna Ashram Marg, 6 A.M.-10 P.M. daily, free) was inaugurated by Gandhi in 1939, who requested that it be open to people of all castes and religions (many Indian temples restrict foreigners, non-Hindus, or "low-caste" people from entry). This three-story temple is built in the North Indian Nagura style, with its signature conical rooftop. The temple houses idols of Lakshmi, goddess of wealth, and her consort, Narayan, an avatar of Vishnu, as well as shrines to a smattering of other deities, including the Buddha. The temple is surrounded by a small park that has a number of colorful plaster animals large enough for children to climb on. Note that photography is not allowed inside the complex, but there's a special section for foreign visitors at the entrance with secure lockers and a shoe area.

the evenings when families flock here to eat ice cream and play on the monument's large lawns. There's also a small artificial lake with pedal boats for hire, although on hot days local boys descend on the lake to roughhouse and get a bit of relief from the heat.

Jantar Mantar

Although it's not nearly as impressive as its sibling in Jaipur, Delhi's Jantar Mantar (Parliament St., Connaught Place, Metro: Patel Chowk, sunrise-sunset Tues.-Sun., Rs. 100 foreigners, Rs. 5 Indians, video Rs. 25) is still worth a visit if you are in the Connaught Place area. The Jantar Mantar was built by Maharaja Sawai Jai Singh II of Jaipur in 1724 and is the first of five similar sights the king built across the northern plains. It is essentially a collection of oversize tools used to make astrological measurements, including the heart-shaped Samrat Yantra (Supreme Instrument) sundial and the Mishra Yantra (Mixed Instrument), a

Lodi Gardens

The beautiful 36-hectare Lodi Gardens (Lodhi Rd., just east of Aurobindo Marg, Metro: Jor Bagh, sunrise-sunset daily, free) is popular with joggers, dog walkers, and young couples and is one of Delhi's best-maintained green areas. There are a variety of birds and trees, and it's popular with picnickers and Frisbee players. It's also home to four tombs. The first of these is the

15th century mausoleum of Muhammad Shah, an octagonal tomb crowned with a large central dome. There's a total of eight graves in this tomb. The second tomb is the Bara Gumbad, and the identity of the person interred here is unknown, although he is believed to have been an officer under Sikandar Lodi's reign. A 15th-century mosque adjoins the tomb. North of the Bara Gumbad, the double-storied Shish Gumbad looks a lot like the Bara Gumbad and contains several graves, although once again, nobody knows whose graves they are. At the northwestern corner of the gardens lies the tomb of Sikandar Lodi himself, which is surrounded by a square garden enclosed in high walls.

National Gallery of Modern Art

Delhi's government-run National Gallery of Modern Art (Jaipur House, C-Hexagon, India Gate, http://ngmaindia.gov.in, 10 A.M.-5 P.M. Tues.-Sun., Rs. 150 foreigners, Rs. 10 Indians)

houses a collection of paintings and sculptures from 1850 onward. The museum was inaugurated in 1954 at Jaipur House, the former residence of the Maharaja of Jaipur. Along with the permanent collection of primarily Indian works, the museum also hosts special exhibitions year-round and occasionally screens films and organizes cultural events. There's also a library and a small gift shop selling postcards and print reproductions of some of the museum's more celebrated pieces.

National Handicrafts and Handlooms Museum

Designed to resemble a rural village, the National Handicrafts and Handlooms Museum (Pragati Maidan, Bhairon Rd., Metro: Pragati Maidan, tel. 11/2337-1887, www.nationalhandicraftsmuseum.nic.in, 10 A.M.-5 P.M. Tues.-Sun., Rs. 150 foreigners, Rs. 10 Indians) houses collections of ethnic and folk art, ritual

© DHRUBA DUTTA

Worshippers chant at Nizamuddin Dargah.

© RAJAT DEEP RANA

Humayan's Tomb is the earliest major example of Mughal architecture in Delhi.

art, sculpture, and textiles. The government-run museum also doubles as a research center for scholars of the traditional arts. The rest of us can enjoy the on-site craft demonstrations, including pottery and hand weaving, just in front of the museum. The gift shop is fabulous and stocks a wide selection of high-quality souvenirs as well as art supplies ranging from pottery tools to locally inspired paint-by-number kits.

National Museum

Delhi's best-known museum, the National Museum (tel. 11/2301-9272, www.nation-almuseumindia.gov.in, 10 A.M.-5 P.M. Tues.-Sun., Rs. 300 foreigners, includes audio tour, Rs. 10 Indians, camera Rs. 20) is home to some 200,000 separate artifacts and works of art from around the world, some of which are believed to be 5,000 years old. The museum has large collections of artifacts from the Harappan lization, armory, miniature paintings, s, textiles, and musical instruments. There

is also a selection of artifacts from India's culturally distinct northeastern states, including costumes, masks, and tools used in everyday life. There's a large wooden chariot here from South India that weighs almost 2,300 kilograms.

National Rail Museum

If you're into trains, don't miss the National Rail Museum (Rao Tula Marg, Chanakyapuri, tel. 11/2688-1816, 9:30 A.M.-5:30 P.M. Tues.-Sun., Rs. 20 adults, Rs. 10 children, video Rs. 100). This museum has everything from model trains (including one of India's first train) to documents that help illustrate the history of India's railroads as well as old railcars, a fire engine, old equipment, and exhibits illustrating how trains work. There is even a working train on the museum grounds, the *Joy Express,* which gives visitors the chance to experience a short train ride.

◖ Nizamuddin Dargah

Nizamuddin Dargah (Mathura Rd.,

© MARGOT BIGG
Safdarjung's Tomb

tradition of Persia that came to India in the 11th century and was developed into a distinct art form in the 13th century by Amir Khusro, a devotee of Nizamuddin. Note that it can get really crowded and stuffy here during Qawwali performances, so turn up early to find a patch of floor and bring a fan and plenty of water unless you're visiting in the dead of winter. You'll also need to leave your shoes at a repository near the entrance to the shrine. Head coverings are not required, but most women prefer to use them as a mark of respect. Male devotees often don a *taqiyah,* or skull cap, available at many of the stalls that flank the walkway to the shrine.

◖ Humayun's Tomb

Set on the grounds of a well-manicured Mughal garden, Humayun's Tomb (Mathura Rd., Nizamuddin East, sunrise-sunset Tues.-Sun., Rs. 250 foreigners, Rs. 10 Indians, video Rs. 25) is the final resting place of Humayun, son of Babur, founder of the Mughal Empire. The tomb, now a UNESCO World Heritage Site, was commissioned by Humayun's widow in the 1570s or 1580s and is considered the first major example of true Mughal architecture. It is also the oldest double-domed structure in India. Along with Humayun, two of his wives and a number of other Mughal rulers are buried in the dank interior of the tomb. The last Mughal emperor, Bahadur Shah II, was captured here by a British lieutenant during the 1857 Indian Rebellion. The tomb itself is interesting (although it is a bit dark inside), and the raised platform it sits on affords good views of Delhi, but the real highlight of this sight is the sprawling gardens complete with pretty fountains.

The same compound is also home to a number of other tombs. To the southeast of the main building sits a double-domed square tomb known as the Barber's Tomb, although nobody really knows who is buried here. The same applies to the blue-domed Nila Gumbad, which,

Nizamuddin West, 24 hours daily, free) is the marble, lattice-screened *dargah* (shrine) of Nizamuddin Auliya, a famous Sufi saint of the Chishti order who lived in Delhi in the 13th and 14th centuries. It is a holy place for Muslims, and there's always a stream of visitors. The present structure was built in 1563 and is essentially a square chamber surrounded by verandas. Although the *dargah* is the main attraction, it's equally fun to simply wander the tiny lanes in Nizamuddin West, the highly traditional, predominantly Muslim neighborhood around the shrine. The area seems like it could have been plucked from another century, especially if you compare this part of Nizamuddin to the ultraposh neighborhoods surrounding it.

Most people try to plan their visit for Thursday evenings around sunset, when a lively session of Qawwali, a form of Sufi devotional music that was popularized in the West by Pakistani musician Nusrat Fateh Ali Khan, is held. Qawwali has its roots in the Sema musical unusually, does not have a double dome. There is debate on when this tomb was built and who is buried here; some believe it may even predate Humayun's mausoleum. The Arab Sarai adjoining the southwestern corner of Humayun's Tomb is believed to have been built to house 300 mullahs (priests) brought from Mecca by Humayun's widow. Others believe it was simply the house of the craftsmen who built the tomb.

Purana Qila

The Purana Qila (Mathura Rd. and Bhairon Marg, Metro: Pragati Maidan, sunrise-sunset Tues.-Sun., Rs. 100 foreigners, Rs. 5 Indians, video Rs. 25, sound and light show Rs. 80 adults, Rs. 40 children), or Old Fort, sits on a mound that is believed to contain the ruins of the ancient city of Indraprastha. Part of the site has been excavated, and the subsequent archaeological findings—Painted Grey Ware pottery from the first millennium B.C.—seem to support this theory. The site was also once the location of the city of Dinpanah, built by

Humayun and destroyed by Sher Shah Suri, founder of the brief Sur Empire and a major rival of the Mughals, who then built a citadel here. It is believed that Sher Shah was unable to finish the project, and Humayun ended up finishing it. Interesting features of the fort include the Qal'a-i-Kuhna-Masjid, a beautiful mosque featuring marble and stone inlay and plenty of high arches and oriel windows. The mosque mixes elements popular in Lodi and Mughal design and is considered significant in that it marks the transition between the two architectural styles. South of the mosque is the Sher Manda, a two-story tower crowned with an octagonal pavilion. It is believed to have been used as a recreational place by Sher Shah and as a library by Humayun. Humayun died here, after falling down the stairs and cracking his head.

Safdarjung's Tomb

Safdarjung was the viceroy of Awadh under Mughal emperor Muhammad Shah. His tomb (Aurobindo Marg and Lodhi Rd., Metro: Jor Bagh, sunrise–sunset Tues.-Sun., Rs. 100 foreigners, Rs. 5 Indians, video Rs. 25), dating from 1754, is the youngest of Delhi's enclosed garden tombs, and its layout is based on the much grander Humayun's Tomb. Its 28-square-meter garden is built in the *char bagh* (four-quarter) style popular in Mughal gardens, although unfortunately it hasn't been very well maintained and is somewhat muddy or dusty, depending on whether you visit in the wet or dry season. A reflecting pool, now empty, leads up to the structure. The interior of the tomb looks like a Jell-O mold and has beautiful carved floral designs on the ceiling. Interestingly, the red stone and marble used to build the tomb was removed from the mausoleum of Khan-i-Khana, near Humayun's Tomb.

THE UNKNOWN TOMBS OF GREEN PARK

Delhi's leafy Green Park neighborhood is home to a few old tombs that are rarely visited by travelers, probably because little is known about their history. These include Bagh-i-Alam Ka Gumbad, a square tomb built in the Lodi style in 1501 A.D. Just up the road from Hauz Khas Village is a small collection of Lodi Tombs; although there is little information as to when they were built or who is buried in them, they are often referred to as the tombs of Dadi and Poti (grandmother and granddaughter). There are plenty of other tombs in the neighborhood, most of which are in the middle of quiet residential streets; again, little is known about their history.

Tibet House Museum

Anyone interested in Tibetan history and culture will not want to miss the Tibet House

The Baha'i House of Worship is often called the Lotus Temple.

Museum (1 Institutional Area, Lodhi Rd., tel. 11/2461-1515, http://tibethousenewdelhi.org, 9:30 A.M.-5:30 P.M. Mon.-Fri., Rs. 10). Tibet House was established by the Dalai Lama in 1965 in order to preserve the cultural heritage of his people after their country was occupied by the Chinese; India is home to their government in exile. The museum houses one of the world's finest collections of *thangkas* (devotional scroll paintings of religious themes) as well as art, costumes, and ritual artifacts. Tibet House also hosts a range of educational activities, including discourses on dharma and music workshops.

SOUTH DELHI
◖ Baha'i House of Worship (Lotus Temple)

Often referred to as the Lotus Temple due to its lotus shape (check it out in satellite images if you get a chance), the Baha'i House of Worship (Kalkaji, Metro: Nehru Place, Kalkaji Mandir, tel. 11/2647-0526, www.bahaihouseofworship. in, 9 A.M.-7 P.M. Tues.-Sun., free) is a peaceful place for prayer and reflection for people of all faiths. It's worth a visit not just for its tranquil ambiance but also for its architectural impressiveness. This beautiful temple was built in the 1980s based on blueprints drawn up by Persian Canadian architect Fariborz Sahba. Sahba traveled across India to draw inspiration for the temple, and he took both Indian symbolism and India's climate into account when developing the concept for the structure. The idea was to craft the temple in the form of a lotus, a symbol of divinity in many eastern religions. Although the temple's architecture is most stunning when seen from the outside, it's also quite impressive from within. The furnishings are on the plain side, but the lotus-shaped skylight at the pinnacle of the temple's ceiling is worth craning your neck to see.

Almost 3.5 million people visit the site every year, and while it's usually a bit crowded, only

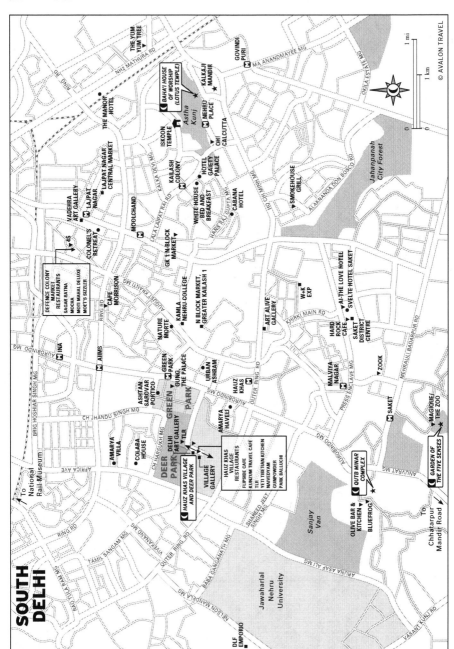

SOUTH DELHI

© AVALON TRAVEL

a select number of people are allowed in the temple's main prayer hall at any given time, and the staff does an incredible job at managing logistics. You must remove your shoes before entering the temple and maintain complete silence. The only time people speak inside is during the five-minute prayer services (10 A.M., noon, 3 P.M., and 5 P.M. daily). Photography is not allowed inside the prayer hall.

Chhatarpur Mandir Road

Those interested in temple architecture and Hinduism won't want to miss a visit to the temple-flanked stretch of Chhatarpur Mandir Road between MG Road and the Chattarpur Mandir (Metro: Chattarpur), also known as Gadaipur Mandi Road. Approaching from the Chhatarpur Metro station on MG Road, you'll notice that the first 500 meters or so of this road is lined with amazing temples and ashrams, including the most famous sight, the Shri Adhya

© RAJAT DEEP RANA

a whimsical tree of bells in the Garden of the Five Senses

Katyani Shakti Peeth Mandir (commonly referred to as the Chattarpur Mandir). This massive white marble temple was built in the 1970s and blends northern and southern Indian architectural styles. Although images of a number of gods and goddesses appear, the primary deity is Katyayani, an avatar of the goddess Durga. If you visit in the evenings during the nine-night festival of Navratri (Sept.-Oct.), the entire street is decorated with tiny multicolored lights.

◖ Garden of the Five Senses

The beautiful Garden of the Five Senses (Said-ul-Ajaib, Mehrauli-Badarpur Rd., tel. 11/2953-6401, 9 A.M.-7 P.M. daily Apr.-Sept., 9 A.M.-6 P.M. daily Oct.-Mar., Rs. 20 adults, Rs. 10 children) occupies an eight-hectare site and is run by Delhi's tourism department. The park is laid out to stimulate the five senses, hence its name, and the flowers and installations are arranged to create a full sensory experience. There are a number of small boutiques as well as a few world-class alfresco restaurants.

The property is split into a number of small gardens, including the Khas Bagh, a model Mughal garden featuring fountains that are gorgeously lit at night by fiber-optic lights. The color gardens feature a number of blooming perennials alongside cacti and other unusual plants. The entire garden is sprinkled with beautiful sculptures, and there's a large amphitheater that regularly hosts plays and concerts. Delhi's Garden Tourism Festival is held here every February.

◖ Hauz Khas Village and Deer Park

One of the most popular hangout spots for expats and artsy Delhiites, Hauz Khas Village (off Aurobindo Marg, just north of Outer Ring Rd., most shops 11 A.M.-7 or 8 P.M. daily), often abbreviated HKV (Delhiites love abbreviations), is worth a visit not only for its many good restaurants and trendy independent boutiques but also for the Lodi-era monuments in the adjoining Deer Park. Although the village has been

the ISKCON Temple in South Delhi

features, is also located in the complex, and he is buried here along with his son and grandson.

ISKCON Temple

The Delhi base of the International Society for Krishna Consciousness (ISKCON), also known as the Hare Krishnas, the ISKCON Temple (Sant Nagar, east of Kailash, tel. 11/2623-5133, www. iskcondelhi.com, 4:30 A.M.-1 P.M. and 4:15-9 P.M. daily, free) is an interesting spot to learn more about the life of Lord Krishna and ISKCON's mission. The temple was built in the 1990s by acclaimed Indian architect Achyut P. Kanvinde and opened to the public in 1998. It's dedicated to Radha and Krishna (although iconography of other deities, as well as ISKCON's founder, Swami Prabhupada, can also be found). There are a couple of small shops on the temple grounds that stock books, religious memorabilia, and CDs of devotional music. The temple's delicious vegetarian restaurant, Govinda's, is reason enough to visit.

Kalkaji Mandir

Not far from the Lotus and ISKCON Temples, the Kalkaji Mandir (Kalkaji Flyover, Outer Ring Rd., Metro: Kalkaji Mandir, 4 A.M.-3 P.M. and 4 P.M.-midnight daily, free) is dedicated to the goddess Kali. A temple is believed to have stood here since the third century B.C., although the current structure dates from the 18th century. The temple is very popular with devotees and travelers, so you may have to wait in long lines and deal with a bit of pushing and shoving. The covered pathway leading up to the temple is flanked with stalls selling sweets and flowers as offerings, and it is customary to present something to the goddess when you enter. Interestingly, the temple is not run by a single priest or clan but by different families who take over the duties of temple maintenance and performing *pujas* (rituals) here on a monthly rotational basis.

◀ Qutb Minar Complex

Among Delhi's most iconic sites, the

undergoing gentrification for many years, there has been a real surge in the area's development lately, and dozens of restaurants have set up in the last few years.

Deer Park gets its name from a large caged-in area that doubles as a deer sanctuary. Some of the deer are astonishingly comfortable with humans, and although it's against the rules, plenty of visitors like to offer the animals grass and other treats through the gates. A popular drum circle is held near the gates every two weeks, usually on Saturday.

At the other end of the park is a collection of monuments next to an enormous tank that was built by Alauddin Khilji (1296-1316) to collect water for his nearby city of Siri. The tank later dried up but was restored by Feroz Shah in the latter part of the 14th century. Feroz Shah also set up a madrassa (religious college) here, the mazelike ruins of which are popular with college students to this day. The ruler's tomb, which blends Indian and Islamic structural

Priests bless devotees at Kalkaji Mandir.

towering Qutb Minar (west of Aurobindo Marg, Mehrauli, Metro: Qutb Minar, sunrise-sunset Tues.-Sun., Rs. 250 foreigners, Rs. 10 Indians, video Rs. 25) is one of Delhi's oldest historic sites. It stretches 72.5 meters into the sky, has 379 steps, and is the highest tower in India. Construction of the Qutb commenced at the end of the 12th century under the reign of Qutb-ud-din Aibak, and it is believed to have been built either as a tower of victory or as a high spot from which people could be called to prayer at the nearby **Quwwatu'l-Islam Mosque.** This mosque was built between 1192 and 1198, and is the oldest extant mosque in India after the pre-sultanate monuments in Kutch, Gujarat. The mosque features a beautifully carved screen featuring geometric patterns and Islamic inscriptions.

Just next to the mosque stands the 7.2-meter-high **Iron Pillar,** believed to date back to the Gupta Dynasty in the late 4th century due to its Sanskrit inscriptions in the Gupta script; it is thought to have been brought to the complex from elsewhere. A third tower, the unfinished Alai Minar, also stands on the complex. It was built by Alauddin Khilji, who had planned for it to be double the size of the Qutb Minar. He had also doubled the size of the mosque, so it's assumed he wanted his tower to be proportionate. Unfortunately, he died before it could be completed, and nobody bothered to carry on where he'd left off.

Another interesting feature of the complex is the **Alai Darwaza,** a domed pavilion with interiors that are a few degrees cooler than the outside temperature (that means a lot in Delhi's summer months). The gateway is made of red sandstone and is one of India's earliest examples of strictly Islamic architecture. Just beyond the Alai Darwaza sits the slightly run-down tomb of an imam from Turkestan by the name of Zamin. This tiny octagonal tomb was built in the 16th century and features beautiful, perforated screens and a large sandstone dome. Like

© MARGOT BIGG

the innovative Sulabh International Museum of Toilets

the Alai Darwaza, the temperatures inside are remarkably cool.

You'll definitely want to block out at least an hour to explore the grounds. The complex is spacious, the gardens are kept in great shape, and there's a lot of open space to move around, so it never feels too crowded. It's also fairly close to the airport, and the low-flying aircraft passing over the towering Qutb Minar make for some great photo ops.

Sulabh International Museum of Toilets

Consistently nominated as one of the world's strangest museums, the Sulabh International Museum of Toilets (Sulabh Bhawan, Mahavir Enclave, Palam Dabri Marg, tel. 11/2503-6122, www.sulabhtoiletmuseum.org, 10 A.M.-5 P.M. Mon.-Sat., free) is as fascinating as it is unusual. The small museum hall is packed with latrines and urinals from around the world along with information about the history of the toilet and

advances in sanitation practices over the years. It may sound gimmicky, but the goal is actually to raise awareness about the often overlooked need for adequate sanitation.

The museum is run by the Sulabh International Service Organization, a nonprofit that helps provide much-needed sanitation services and waste recycling technology to India's most needy. The people at Sulabh are experts at converting human excreta into biogas and extracting contaminants from urine, essentially converting it to water that can be safely used for irrigation. The staff is very friendly and eager to assist visitors, and it's easy to get someone to explain how the toilets and related waste conversion processes work. Ask to see the staff kitchen—the stove they use runs entirely on biogas sourced from human waste.

NORTH DELHI
Majnu Ka Tilla Tibetan Enclave
The small Tibetan enclave of Majnu Ka

Tilla (near the Majnu Ka Tilla Gurudwara, Mahatma Gandhi Rd., Metro: Vidhan Sabha) is primarily home to Tibetan people who were no longer able to stay in their native land after the Chinese invaded. It's a popular alternative to Paharganj among the backpacker set, but it's quite far from town, and the quality of accommodations is not good enough to get a recommendation in this book. The colony, however, is worth a visit if you're interested in Tibetan culture, and there are plenty of shops and eateries selling Tibetan (and, ironically, Chinese) products and food. The main square is home to the local Tibetan monastery, which features a massive prayer wheel on its stoop as well as a number of smaller wheels flanking its sides. Devotees customarily circumambulate the building in the clockwise direction, spinning each wheel as they pass by.

EAST DELHI
Swaminarayan Akshardham Complex

Delhi's newest major attraction, the Swaminarayan Akshardham Complex (Gurjar Samrat Mir Bhoj Marg and Noida Link Rd., Metro: Akshardham, tel. 11/2201-6688, www.akshardham.com, 9:30 A.M.-6:30 P.M. Mon.-Sat., free) officially opened in 2005 and is named after Bhagwan Swaminarayan, founder of the Swaminarayan sect of Hinduism. At the center of the complex sits a 33-meter-tall, intricately carved temple dedicated to Swaminarayan made entirely of pink sandstone (6,000 tons of it, no less). The temple features beautifully carved screens, bas-reliefs, and pillars, including four that, at 10 meters, are the tallest in the country. Other popular attractions on the site include the fabulously cheesy audio-animatronics show (think a higher-tech version of a robotics show, like the Pirates of the Caribbean ride at Disneyland). *Mystic India,* a film that retells the fascinating true-life story of an 11-year-old yogi who traveled across the country in search of spiritual truth, is also screened. The complex is home to several other exhibits and experiences, including sound and light shows, interactive fiber-optic installations, and displays of scenes from some of India's greatest epic tales.

Entertainment and Events

Delhi is a fairly festive place, and there's usually something going on, be it a religious festival, a fashion week, a convention, or an international sporting event. It also has a lively arts scene, arguably unparalleled anywhere else in the country, and lovers of the fine and performing arts will find plenty going on. Delhi also has a growing nightlife scene, and on most nights you'll be able to choose from a number of places to go out dancing.

NIGHTLIFE

Delhi's nightlife scene is growing, and a number of new and successful bars and nightclubs open every year. Most are required to close by 1 A.M., although club owners often find ways of getting special permission to go on until the wee hours. The official drinking age in clubs and bars is 25, although this is rarely enforced. Most have dress codes, and men without close-toed shoes may be denied entry. Others prohibit stag (single-male) entry, so call ahead to check, or make sure you have a woman for every man in your group.

The most popular types of music among Delhi's youth are the ubiquitous Bollywood film songs, followed by Punjabi bhangra music. Rock music is a close third, and India has a thriving homegrown rock music scene. If you're interested in electronic dance music, it's a good idea to check what's going on ahead of time. Club listings can be found in the Nightlife section of *Time Out* magazine. Also note that things change really fast in the capital, and today's hot club may be shut down permanently tomorrow (the city's bureaucratic Excise Commission, responsible for issuing alcohol licenses, doesn't help things much). The venues listed below are pretty well established and are likely to be around for many years to come.

Nicknamed "the press club" for its popularity with Delhi journalists, **4S** (A-26 Defence Colony Market, tel. 11/4166-4314, noon–midnight daily, no cover) is Delhi's most beloved dive bar, partially because the 50-percent-off happy hour at this already cheap bar lasts until 10 P.M. 4S is what is known in India as a resto-bar, and they serve up a great selection of deep-fried Chinese snacks, which taste great after a few beers. The doorman, with his long mustache and perpetual smile, makes the place feel incredibly welcoming, whether you're a first-time customer or a tipsy regular.

One of the newest clubs in Delhi, **blueFROG** (The Kila, Seven Style Mile, opposite Qutb Minar, Mehrauli, tel. 11/2664-5298, www.blue-frog.co.in, 8 A.M.–1 A.M. Tues.–Sun., cover after 8 P.M. Sat., after 9 P.M. Sun.–Fri., charge varies) opened at the end of 2011 and has already become a popular place to dance the night away. Modeled after its flagship club in Mumbai, Delhi's blueFROG offers modern interiors and a great selection of cocktails. They regularly host bands and DJs from across India and abroad.

Rock is not dead at **Café Morrison** (E-12 South Extension II Market, tel. 9810/261-442, www.cafemorrison.com, noon–1 A.M. daily); in fact, it's celebrated with verve at this multistory bar decorated with rock posters. Café Morrison is popular with college students, who come to get drunk and listen to *Smells Like Teen Spirit* at full blast. If that doesn't sound like your idea of a, um, rocking time, you can always hang out on the top floor, which regularly hosts DJs.

The fashionable **F-Bar** (The Ashok, 50, Chanakyapuri, tel. 11/2611-1119, www.fbardelhi.com, 24 hours daily, from Rs. 2,000, couples only) is good for people-watching, throwing away vast amounts of money, and general ostentation. The cover charge is expensive, and the main draw of this little place is that it never closes (although the DJs do eventually go home). F-Bar occasionally host some amazing major artists from India and abroad, which attract a good crowd of happy, dancing people.

Ever heard of tinnitus, that unceasing ringing in your ears that's often caused by operating loud machinery without ear protection? If not, you'll know all about it after a visit to **Hard Rock Café** (M-110, Multiplex Bldg., 1st Fl., DLF Place, Saket District Centre, tel. 11/4715-8888, www.hardrock.com, noon–1 A.M. daily, cover charge for some performance nights), where the decibels are pushed up far beyond reasonable limits. The Delhi branch of this international institution hosts some great bands every once in a while. The rest of the time, they blast really loud rock music. Like all venues in Delhi, it's nonsmoking, although they do have an unventilated aquarium-like smoking room. The burgers and ice cream sundaes are delicious.

Connaught Place's **Q'ba** (Radial No 7, E Block, Connaught Place, tel. 11/4517-3333, noon–1 A.M. daily, no cover) is a spacious, reasonably-priced bar-restaurant right in the middle of town. It's more a drinking spot than a place to dance, although they occasionally host events, and it's popular with the after-work crowd.

Rick's (Taj Mahal Hotel, 1 Mansingh Rd., tel. 11/6651-3246, 12:30 P.M.–1 A.M. Sun.–Thurs., 12:30 P.M.–2 A.M. Fri.–Sat., no cover) is a small, quite chic hotel bar that attracts a fun-loving set of big spenders. It's cozy, and the music is not played at full blast, although it's still loud enough to get down on the small dance floor.

Delhi's wealthy over-30 set flock to **Smokehouse Grill** (2 VIPPS Center, LSC Masjid Moth, Greater Kailash II, tel.

11/4143-5531, http://smokehousegrill.in, 7:30 P.M.-1 A.M. daily, no cover most nights). This double-story restaurant serves excellent cocktails, and there's usually a DJ playing commercial house music. It's a friendly place, and most of the guests are on the social side. Note that the dress code is strictly enforced.

An expat favorite, **TLR** (31 Hauz Khas Village, Metro: Green Park, tel. 11/4608-0533, www.tlrcafe.com, 11 A.M.-midnight daily, no cover) hosts regular open mike and themed dance music events, where everything from animal masks to sparkly pom-poms are distributed to the audience. It's a convivial place with frequent specials on beer (often two-for-one). They also serve food, and the dress code is a bit more casual than many other places in Delhi.

In the enchanting Garden of the Five Senses, **The Zoo** (Garden of Five Senses, Said-Ul-Ajaib, Mehrauli, tel. 11/6557-6198, 7 P.M.-1 A.M. daily, no cover most nights) is a popular nightspot featuring primarily electronic music DJs. There's a small dance floor indoors, but guests tend to congregate in the enclosed outdoor area, where it's a bit easier to have a conversation. There's rarely a cover charge, and there is usually no problem for single men to gain entry; nice shoes are a must.

Part hookah bar, part restaurant, **Zook** (No. 3 PVR Anupam Complex, Saket, tel. 11/4105-7482, noon-1 A.M. daily, no cover most nights) hosts some interesting events, including reggae parties put on by Delhi's Reggae Rajahs as well as drum-and-bass and dubstep nights by local sound system BASSFoundation. The interiors are modern and incorporate light wood with colorful posters, including a corny pointillist version of the iconic shirtless photo of Jim Morrison.

THE ARTS
Art Galleries
Although it has only been around for a bit over a decade, South Delhi's **Art Alive Gallery** (S-221 Panchsheel Marg, tel. 11/4163-9000, www.

artalivegallery.com, 11 A.M.-7 P.M. Mon.-Sat.) has made a tremendous contribution to India's art scene. This gallery focuses on contemporary Indian art and is active in promoting Indian art on the international scene. There's a second branch in the nearby city of Gurgaon.

Delhi Art Gallery (11 Hauz Khas Village, tel. 11/4600-5300, http://delhiartgallery.com, 11 A.M. to 7 P.M. Mon.-Sat.) has a huge collection of pieces from Indian modernists. Appraisal and authentication services are also offered, and the knowledgeable staff can help those who are new to buying art or are unfamiliar with Indian art.

Named for the French term for still life, **Nature Morte** (A-1, opposite Kamla Nehru College, Niti Bagh, tel. 11/4174-0215, www.naturemorte.com, 10 A.M.-6 P.M. Mon.-Sat.) exhibits a variety of modern art from established artists. This basement gallery is run by Peter Negi, one of India's best-known curators. There are additional branches in Gurgaon and Berlin.

One of the best-known and most respected galleries in the capital, **Vadehra Art Gallery** (D-40 Defence Colony, Metro: Lajpat Nagar, tel. 11/2462-2545, http://vadehraart.com, 10:30 A.M.-7 P.M. Mon.-Sat.) has exhibited work from India's best-known modern artists. The gallery is home to the Foundation for Indian Contemporary Art and even has its own publishing branch.

It has been over 20 years since **Village Gallery** (14 Hauz Khas Village, Metro: Green Park, tel. 11/2685-3860, http://thevillagegallery.co.in, 2:30-7 P.M. Mon.-Sat.) first opened its doors in South Delhi's artsy Hauz Khas Village. The gallery continues to exhibit art from established and up-and-coming Indian artists to this day.

The official Delhi gallery of Oregon advertising behemoth Wieden+Kennedy (the people who coined the phrase "Just Do It" for Nike), **W+K Exp** (B-10 DDA Complex, Sheikh Sarai Phase I, Metro: Malviya Nagar, tel. 11/4600-9595, www.wkdelhiblog.com, 10 A.M.-7 P.M. Mon.-Sat.) hosts rotating exhibitions from Indian and international artists.

Cinemas

There are literally hundreds of cinemas in Delhi, ranging from dinky little places that screen the same old Bollywood film week after week to ultramodern multiplexes. **Regal Cinema** (Connaught Place, tel. 11/2336-2245, Metro: Rajiv Chowk) is Connaught Place's best-known movie hall, although it's not as nice as some of the newer venues. PVR Cinemas (various locations, www.pvrcinemas.com) operate the vast majority of Delhi's newer high-quality cinemas and consistently screens English-language films. Other cinema companies include Satyam Cineplexes (various locations, www.satyamcineplexes.com) and M2K Cinemas (various locations, www.m2kcinemas.com).

Cultural Centers

The main focus of the **Alliance Française** (72 Lodhi Estate, Connaught Place, tel. 11/5101-2091, http://delhi.afindia.org, 9 A.M.-6 P.M. Mon.-Sat.), the French cultural center, is imparting French language skills on those who care to learn, but it also hosts a wide range of cultural events and lectures, usually with a French touch. There's also a small theater and an art gallery.

The Attic (36 Regal Bldg., Connaught Place, Metro: Rajiv Chowk, tel. 11/2374-6050, http://theatticdelhi.org, open only for events) was set up with the goal of preserving and showcasing textiles and heirlooms, but they do much more. This Connaught Place gallery hosts regular talks, recitals, and concerts on a wide range of topics and by a diverse group of performers.

Painted to look like a black-and-white cow, the **British Council** (17 Kasturba Gandhi Marg, Connaught Place, Metro: Barakhamba Rd., tel. 11/2371-1401, www.britishcouncil.org, 9 A.M.-5 P.M. Mon.-Fri.) sponsors a wide range of cultural activities aimed at strengthening the Indo-British relationship. Events are occasionally held in the courtyard.

Germany's cultural center, the **Goethe Institute/Max Mueller Bhawan** (3 Kasturba Gandhi Marg, Connaught Place, Metro: Barakhamba Rd., tel. 11/2332-9506, www.goethe.de/newdelhi, 9:30 A.M.-6 P.M. Mon.-Fri.) plays host to a great number of cultural events on its spacious lawns and in its indoor performance area. Performers, especially electronic musicians, are regularly brought from Germany.

The massive **India Habitat Centre** (Lodhi Rd, Lodhi Estate, Lodhi Colony, tel. 11/2468-2001, http://indiahabitat.org, 8 A.M.-9 P.M. daily) holds a wide variety of musical performances, art exhibitions, lectures, and film screenings. A number of government and nongovernmental organizations also have branches here.

Just up the road from the Habitat Centre, the **India International Centre** (40 Lodhi Rd., Max Mueller Marg, Connaught Place, tel. 11/2461-9431, http://iicdelhi.nic.in, 10 A.M.-5 P.M. daily) hosts similar events, ranging from classical music performances to talks from some of India's finest scholars.

Theaters and Auditoriums

Plays are staged at one of the many theaters in Central Delhi's Mandi House area. You can see plays performed in both English and Hindi. Prices vary depending on the performance, but ticket prices usually range from Rs.100-500. Theaters include the National School of Drama's **Abhimanch Auditorium** (1 Bhagwan Das Rd., Pragati Maidan, Metro: Mandi House, tel. 11/2338-2821, www.nsd.gov.in), **Kamani Auditorium** (1 Copernicus Marg, Connaught Place, Metro: Mandi House, tel. 11/4350-3351, www.kamaniauditorium.org), **The Little Theatre Group Auditorium** (Copernicus Marg, near Barakhamba Rd., Metro: Mandi House, tel. 11/2338-9713), **Meghdoot Theatre** (Rabindra Bhawan, Copernicus Marg, Mandi House, Metro: Mandi House, tel. 11/2338-7241), and the **Shri Ram Centre for Performing Arts** (4 Safdar Hashmi Marg, Metro: Mandi House, tel. 11/2371-4307, www. shriramcenterart.org), which has its own repertory company. Call ahead or check local papers for showtimes and ticket prices.

FESTIVALS AND EVENTS
Bharat Rang Mahotsav
The largest theater festival in Delhi, the National School of Drama's two-week-long Bharat Rang Mahotsav (www.nsdtheatrefest. com) in January stages dozens of performances in a variety of genres, performed by both local and international theater companies.

Republic Day
Republic Day (www.republicday.nic.in), January 26, is the national holiday that commemorates the Republic of India's constitution. It is observed across India, but nowhere are the celebrations more fervent than in Delhi. In the morning a large parade moves along Rajpath in Central Delhi, featuring floats, military marchers, and even elephant processions.

Garden Tourism Festival
This government-run outdoor garden festival in February takes place at the beautiful Garden of the Five Senses and features gardening demonstrations, lectures on horticulture, a plant and flower market, cultural performances, a bonsai exhibition, and a flower show.

Monsoon Festival
The Monsoon Festival (http://themonsoonfestival.com) is an arts festival is held in honor of the refreshing annual monsoon. It features a wide selection of activities, including art exhibitions, theatrical performances, handicrafts markets, and lectures.

Osian's Cinefan Festival of Asian and Arab Cinema
The Cinefan Festival (www.cinefan.osians. com) is staged in July at multiple venues and celebrates the best in cinema from across Asia and the Arab world with screenings, discussion panels, and film awards.

International Mango Festival
Really more of a convention than a bona fide festival, July's International Mango Festival is dedicated to India's best-loved fruit and features exhibitions, tastings, and cooking demonstrations as well as the opportunity to sample dozens of varieties of this succulent fruit and related products.

Delhi Book Fair
The annual Delhi Book Fair (www.delhibookfair.in), held in August-September, is primarily aimed at people in the publishing industry, but it always ends up attracting nonindustry folk who flock here to check out the latest titles on offer and to pick up discounted books.

Delhi Photo Festival
Held in October in odd-numbered years, the Delhi Photo Festival (www.delhiphotofestival. com) features a wide range of activities, including hands-on photography workshops, lectures, contests, and, naturally, photography exhibitions.

Delhi International Arts Festival
The enormous Delhi International Arts Festival (www.diaf.in) takes place over a couple of weeks in November and is spread over multiple venues around town. The organizers take a comprehensive view of what an arts festival should be, so along with traditional visual and performing arts, the best of literature, film, and even culinary arts are featured.

Qutb Festival
Set against the backdrop of the iconic Qutb Minar, this five-day music festival, held in November or December, features performances from top Indian musicians, ranging from classical artists to popular Hindi film singers.

Shopping

If someone were to hold a contest for India's best shopping city, Delhi would easily win. The capital is filled with shopping options for every budget, from ultralow-cost open-air markets to fancy malls specializing in prêt-à-porter from France and Italy's top designers. It's a great place to buy handicrafts, and while Delhi doesn't have much of a crafts tradition of its own, you can pick up bits and pieces from around the country.

SHOPPING DISTRICTS

There are plenty of good spots to shop in Delhi, some better than others. The most established is Central Delhi's **Connaught Place** (Metro: Rajiv Chowk, most shops Mon.-Sat.), the commercial center of New Delhi and home to a great number of shops selling toys, books, clothing, and housewares. Also in Central Delhi, **Khan Market** (Metro: Khan Market, most shops Mon.-Sat.) is popular with rich Delhiites and embassy staff. It also has one of the highest concentrations of great restaurants in town.

In South Delhi, **Greater Kailash I** (east of Josip Broz Tito Marg, between Lala Lajpat Rai Path and Outer Ring Rd.) is a hugely popular shopping and residential area and is usually referred to simply as "GK." While the M-Block Market here focuses more on Western clothes, appliances, and other items that are not likely to be of much interest to visitors, the N-Block Market just down the road has lots of lovely upscale Indian clothing boutiques as well as a number of slick home furnishings shops. The ultratrendy **Hauz Khas Village** (off Aurobindo Marg, just north of Outer Ring Rd.) is chock-full of cute little independent clothing boutiques, antiques dealers, and art galleries, but gentrification is making it difficult for some artists to sustain their workshops. Many are moving to the much more bohemian village

of **Shahpurjat** just down the road, and this is the place to go for bargain bespoke pieces from up-and-coming young designers.

The epicenter of Old Delhi's commercial activity, the never-boring and usually chaotic **Chandni Chowk** (west of Lal Qila, between Netaji Subhash Rd. and GB Rd., most shops 10 A.M.-8 P.M. Mon.-Sat.) is Delhi's most famous market and a popular place to pick up jewelry, textiles, and *itar* (essential oil). It's also a good place to buy spices, but to be completely honest, the reputable supermarket brands (such as MDH) are generally just as good and are easier to get through customs than unlabeled bulk items.

The market was established in the 17th century by Emperor Shahjahan in what was then the walled city of city of Shahjahanabad. Chandni Chowk is Hindi for Moonlight Square; there was once a canal here positioned to reflect moonlight.

HANDICRAFTS

India has some amazing handicraft items, including beautiful shawls and papier-mâché pieces from Kashmir, silk saris from Varanasi, and mirrored bedspreads from Rajasthan. All of this can be found under one roof at the government-run **Cottage Industries** (Jawahar Vyapar Bhavan, Janpath, Metro: Rajiv Chowk, tel. 11/2332-0439, http://cottageemporium.in, 10 A.M.-7 P.M. daily). This huge showroom sells items from around the country at fixed prices, and although the items are slightly pricier than they might be if you got into a bargaining match with a local vendor, you can be sure of the quality.

Another government-run initiative aimed at promoting regional handicrafts, the **State Emporia Complex** (Baba Kharak Rd., Patel Chowk, Metro: Shivaji Stadium, 11 A.M.-7 P.M. Mon.-Sat.) has shops run by the tourism departments of the various states. You'll find a wide

South Delhi's trendy Hauz Khas Village

range of handicraft items, mostly housewares, arts, and textiles from around the country. Just pick your state of choice and start shopping. You can also find products from around India at the government-run crafts village **Dilli Haat** (Auobindo Marg and Ring Rd., 10:30 A.M.-9 P.M. daily, Rs. 20 adults, Rs. 10 children).

BOUTIQUES

The Delhi outlet of a well-respected Jaipur jewelry shop, **Amarpali** (39-39A Khan Market, Metro: Khan Market, tel. 11/4175-2024, www.amrapalijewels.com, 10:30 A.M.-7:30 P.M. Mon.-Sat., noon-5 P.M. Sun.) features a huge assortment of primarily silver jewelry designs, ranging from traditional Rajashtani enamel pieces to ultracontemporary designs.

For beautiful block-printed women's wear and upholstery, head straight to **Anokhi** (32 Khan Market, Metro: Khan Market, tel. 11/2460-3423, www.anokhi.com, 10 A.M.-8 P.M. daily). This Jaipur institution

is a big hit in Delhi, selling a large range of Indian women's wear as well as dresses, duvet covers, and super-soft cotton pajamas, all made of fine hand-block printed cottons. There's also a branch in Greater Kailash I (N-16 N-Block Market, Greater Kailash I, Metro: Kailash Colony, tel. 11/2923-1500, www.anokhi.com, 10 A.M.-8 P.M. daily).

Flouncy skirts and subtly bejeweled kurtas (tunics) abound at **Cottons** (N-11 Greater Kailash I, Metro: Kailash Colony, tel. 11/4163-5108, 10:30 A.M.-7 P.M. daily). This women's wear shop specializes in ethnic apparel with modern cuts, and it is a great place to pick up the beautiful long scarves, called *dupattas,* that you'll often see Indian women draping around their shoulders.

If you'd like to pick up a few pieces of traditional Indian clothing but don't want anything too shiny or brightly colored, **Fab India** (B-28 Upper Ground Fl., Inner Circle, Connaught Place, Metro: Rajiv Chowk, tel. 11/4151-3371, www.fabindia.com, 11 A.M.-8 P.M. daily) is your best bet. This shop specializes in tunics for men and women made from hand-dyed natural fabrics. They also have a good array of skirts, blouses, stoles, *salwars* (loose trousers) and *churidars* (trousers tapered at the ankles) as well as home furnishings and organic spices. Fab India has branches around India, including one in Greater Kailash (N-14 Greater Kailash I, Metro: Kailash Colony, tel. 11/2923-2183, 10 A.M.-8 P.M. daily) and Khan Market (Middle Lane, above Shop 20-21, Khan Market, Metro: Khan Market, tel. 11/4368-3100, 10 A.M.-8 P.M. daily).

One of the best interior design shops in India, **Good Earth** (9 Khan Market, Metro: Khan Market, tel. 11/2464-7175, www.goodearth.in, 11 A.M.-8:30 P.M. daily) stocks a beautiful array of everything from candles to cutlery, including many designs that blend classical Indian aesthetics with contemporary functionality. There's a small selection of beautiful linen dresses on the second floor.

For high-quality leather goods at a fraction of what you would pay back home, check out **Hidesign** (N-10 Greater Kailash I, Metro: Kailash Colony, tel. 11/2923-6034, http://hidesign.com, 10:30 A.M.-8:30 P.M. daily). The Pondicherry-based company is India's best-known producer of leatherwear, and their products—handbags, wallets, and attaché cases—are sold in department stores around the world. The designs are contemporary and on par with what you might find in Italy. There are outlets across India, including one at Khan Market (49-A Khan Market, Metro: Khan Market, tel. 11/2461-5314, 10 A.M.-8 P.M. daily).

For unique souvenirs, check out **Khazana India** (50-A Haus Khas Village, Metro: Green Park, tel. 11/6469-0579, 10:30 A.M.-8 P.M. daily). This small shop is a perfect place to pick up old advertising posters, magnets, and other aging Indian curios. It also stocks very cool antique candy tins, adorned with images of Indian deities.

Nappa Dori (HKV) (Shop 4, Hauz Khas Village, Metro: Green Park, tel. 9810/400-778, www.nappadori.com, 11:30 A.M.-7:30 P.M. Tues.-Sun.) stocks colorful trunks with stands so that they can double as tables, journals, handbags, billfolds, and toiletry cases featuring sepia-toned scenes from India's past. There's a second showroom a few doors down showcasing additional Nappa Dori items as well as pretty cushion covers and other soft furnishings by local designer Shruti Reddy.

Looking for a gift for someone back home and not sure what to get? **Purple Jungle** (16 Ground Fl., Hauz Khas Village, Metro: Green Park, tel. 11/2653-8182, http://purple-jungle.com, 11 A.M.-7 P.M. daily) just may be the shop you've been searching for. This tiny boutique specializes in brightly colored purses, toiletry cases, cushions, and other gift items made from up-cycled educational posters from India. Additional stock is kept in the studio-warehouse a few doors down—feel free to ask to visit it if you don't find the perfect gift in the main showroom.

BOOKSTORES

A Khan Market favorite, **Bahri Sons** (opposite Main Gate, Khan Market, Metro: Khan Market, tel. 11/2469-4610, www.booksatbahri.com, 10 A.M.-2 P.M. and 2:30-7:30 P.M. Mon.-Sat.) has been selling books to Delhiites for over half a century. They stock a huge variety of fiction titles as well as hundreds of magazines from India and abroad.

You can pick up excellent coffee-table books on India at **Full Circle** (N-16 Greater Kailash I, Metro: Kailash Colony, tel. 11/2924-5643, www.fullcirclebooks.in, 9:30 A.M.-8:30 P.M. daily). Although the art book section is the main draw, there is also a great selection of children's lit, spiritual books, and Indian fiction. There are other branches around Delhi, including one at Khan Market (Shop 23, 1st and 2nd Fl., Middle Lane, Khan Market, Metro: Khan Market, tel. 11/2465-5641, 9:30 A.M.-8:30 P.M. daily).

No book lover should miss **Yodakin**

Bookstore (2 Hauz Khas Village, Metro: Green Park, tel. 11/4178-7201, www.yodakin.com, 11 A.M.-8 P.M. Mon. and Wed.-Sat., 2-8 P.M. Tues., noon-8 P.M. Sun.), a cozy shop specializing in books from independent publishers with plenty of titles that you won't find elsewhere. There's also a large selection of art and design periodicals as well as a small collection of music and films.

MUSICAL INSTRUMENTS

If you'd like to pick up a classical Indian instrument, your two best bets are South Delhi's **Bharat Music House** (B-113 Lajpat Nagar I, Metro: Lajpat Nagar, tel. 11/2981-0212, www.bharatmusichouse.com, 11:30 A.M.-7:30 P.M. Tues.-Sun.) and Connaught Place's **Rikhi Ram** (G-8 Marina Arcade, Connaught Circus, Connaught Place, Metro: Rajiv Chowk, tel. 11/2332-7685, www.rikhiram.com, 12:30-8 P.M. Mon.-Sat.). Both manufacture a wide array of Indian instruments—Rikhi Ram even has miniature versions—and can help you figure out a way to ship instruments home if you don't want to carry them as luggage.

SHOPPING MALLS

Delhi has tons of shopping malls, most of which have a lot of stores similar to what you might find back home. One of the oldest is **Ansal Plaza** (August Kranti Marg, between Ring Rd. and Siri Fort Rd., shop hours vary, mall 11 A.M.-10:30 P.M. daily) in South Delhi. There's a big cluster of malls in South Delhi's Saket neighborhood in a strip known as **Saket District Centre** (Press Enclave Marg, east of Lal Bahadur Shastri Marg, shop hours vary, malls 10 A.M.-11 P.M. daily). The malls, including **Select Citywalk, DLF Place,** and **Metropolitan Mall,** are home to a huge number of cinemas, restaurants, department stores, and chain boutiques. Few visitors to Delhi find any real reason to visit these malls, which stock items that can be found in most of the

Western world at more or less the same prices. Popular shops include Zara, FCUK, Levi's, and Adidas. Designer brands such as Gucci, Jimmy Choo, and Louis Vuitton can be found at **DLF Emporio** (4 Nelson Mandela Marg, Vasant Kunj, shop hours vary, mall 11 A.M.-1 A.M. daily), but because of high import taxes, these items will cost you far more than they would in your home country. The biggest mall in India, **Ambience Mall,** is just outside Delhi in the satellite city of Gurgaon. It features hundreds of shops, a huge food court with a play area, a bowling alley, and a brewery. Gurgaon is home to scores of other malls, all of which stock more or less the same things, namely sportswear, Indian clothes, and shoes. The majority of these malls can be found on Gurgaon's MG Road, accessible via the IFFCO Chowk or MG Road Metro stations.

OUTDOOR MARKETS

Delhi has tons of excellent outdoor markets. For kitchenware and Indian clothes—especially saris—head to busy **Lajpat Nagar Central Market** (Metro: Lajpat Nagar, most shops 10 A.M.-8 P.M. Tues.-Sun.). The market is one of the most congested shopping areas in South Delhi, and entire sections focus on kitchenware, saris, fabric, and shoes. This is also a great place to buy bangles; whole shops are devoted to these beautiful bracelets.

Karol Bagh Market (Pusa Rd. and Arya Samaj Rd., most shops 10 A.M.-8 P.M. Tues.-Sun.) is a bit more convenient if you're coming from Paharganj or Connaught Place. It's similar in many ways to Lajpat Nagar, although it is a bit bigger. Popular buys include saris and jewelry, ranging from costume items to exquisite diamond-studded wedding pieces.

Young women won't want to miss the fabulous deals on surplus clothing at **Sarojini Nagar Market** (Brig Hoshiar Singh Marg, near Africa Ave., most shops 10 A.M.-8 P.M. Tues.-Sun.). India is a major producer of clothing for more developed countries, and the pieces that don't quite make the cut, usually due to a missing button or an inconsistent dye job, are sold here at rock-bottom prices. It's like an open-air version of a factory outlet store, and there is always lot of stuff from H&M, Esprit, FCUK, and Ralph Lauren.

The best deals on hippie gear, Hindu deity statues, tapestries, and costume jewelry are at **Paharganj** (across from New Delhi Railway Station, Qutab Rd., most shops 11 A.M.-8 P.M. Tues.-Sun.) and the **Tibetan Market** (Janpath, near Connaught Place, 11 A.M.-8 P.M. Mon.-Sat.). These two markets cater primarily to visitors, although plenty of Indian college students frequent them too. The goods on offer are inexpensive by Western standards, but most shopkeepers will start with high prices and expect you to bargain them down.

If you'd rather not have to negotiate a price, you'll love **Dilli Haat** (Auobindo Marg and Ring Rd., 10:30 A.M.-9 P.M. daily, Rs. 20 adults, Rs. 10 children). This government-run market features artisans from across the country, and it's a great place to get the feel of a crafts market without the noise and pushy sales pleas that are common in most other markets. It's definitely on the artificial side, but the products here are of good quality. There's also an excellent food court featuring cuisine from across the country, and locals love to come here just to eat.

Sports and Recreation

Delhi is not a typical sports and recreation destination. Most of the sporting infrastructure, including the listings below, are aimed more at locals.

SPORTS FACILITIES

If your hotel doesn't have a gym and you are dying to work out, your best options are South Delhi's two major sports complexes, both of which offer temporary memberships. **Saket Sports Complex** (opposite Welcome Marriott Hotel, Saket, tel. 11/2956-1742, www.dda.org.in, 6:30 A.M.-11:30 P.M. Tues.-Sun., 4-8:30 P.M. Mon., gym Rs. 220 per hour), offers a large number of activities and classes, ranging from tae kwon do to ballroom dancing.

Another popular South Delhi option is the **Siri Fort Sports Complex** (August Kranti Marg, tel. 11/2649-7482, www.dda.org.in, 6 A.M.-9 P.M. daily, rates vary by activity), a sprawling sports facility offering everything from rifle shooting to Reiki. There are also 12 tennis courts on-site.

GOLF

The best place to go for golf in Delhi is the **Delhi Golf Club** (Dr. Zakir Hussain Marg, tel. 11/2430-7100, www.delhigolfclub.org, sunrise-sunset Tues.-Sun., 18 holes Rs. 3,000 Sat.-Sun., Rs. 2,000 Mon.-Fri., 9 holes Rs. 1,250 Sat.-Sun.). The club sits in the heart of central Delhi and comprises the 18-hole Lodhi Course and the 9-hole Peacock Course. A number of old Lodi-era tombs dot the grounds. There's also a pool and a bar on-site.

Delhi is also home to a much more affordable, and not nearly as nice, nine-hole course at **Siri Fort Complex** (August Kranti Marg, tel. 11/2649-7482, www.dda.org.in, 6 A.M.-9 P.M. daily, admission Rs. 40, Rs. 50 for 50 balls). This plain grass golfing facility has a driving range and a pitch-and-putt course.

HORSEBACK RIDING

There aren't many great places to go riding in Delhi, but you can always drop in to one of the lessons at the **Delhi Riding Club** (behind Safdarjung Tomb, Safdarjung Rd., Metro: Jor Bagh, tel. 11/2301-1891, 6:30-8:30 A.M. and 2:45-5:45 P.M. daily, Rs. 800 per adult's class, Rs. 600 per children's class). There are beginner and intermediate hunt-seat lessons (no jumping) for children and adults, and helmets are provided.

SWIMMING

For sport swimming rather than poolside lounging, there's a well-maintained Olympic-size swimming pool at **Siri Fort Sports Complex** (August Kranti Marg, tel. 11/2649-7482, www.dda.org.in, 6 A.M.-9 P.M. daily, Rs. 500). There's a similar pool at **Saket Sports Complex** (opposite Welcome Marriott Hotel, Saket, tel. 11/2956-1742, www.dda.org.in, 6:30 A.M.-11:30 P.M. Tues.-Sun., 4-8:30 P.M. Mon., Rs. 500). Both facilities are government-owned and are run by the Delhi Development Authority. The pool at the **Pacific Sports Complex** (Central School, near Moolchand Flyover, tel. 11/2645-2748, www.pacificsportscomplex.in, 6 A.M.-10 P.M. daily, Rs. 300 per hour) is popular, although it gets quite crowded in summer. Swimming sessions here start every hour on the hour, and at the end of your time slot, an attendant blows a whistle and forces everyone out. Note that a swim cap is required for people with long hair, and bikinis are frowned upon.

For something a bit more relaxed and considerably less sporty, check out the swimming pool at the **Park Hotel** (15 Parliament Rd., tel. 11/2374-3000, www.theparkhotels.com, 7 A.M.-7 P.M. daily, Rs. 700). This small pool is great for sunbathing and short swims, although it's a bit too shallow for diving. There's also a lovely poolside bar and restaurant.

YOGA

Delhi has plenty of places to practice yoga, and most of the five-star hotels and larger gyms offer guided sessions. For something a bit more traditional, drop in to one of the open classes at the **Sivananda Yoga Vedanta Centre** (A-41 Kailash Colony, Metro: Kailash Colony, tel. 11/3206-9070, www.sivananda.org/delhi, 6:30 A.M.-8 P.M. daily, Rs. 300 per class, packages available). The Delhi branch of the worldwide Sivananda Yoga organization offers 90-minute drop-in hatha yoga classes that

concentrate on focusing the mind and opening the spine through breath, self-awareness, and an alternating mix of postures and relaxation. As it is a traditional center, dress modestly; tank tops are fine, but no sports bras or Speedos. If you are a complete beginner, you have to take an introductory course first to learn how to do the asanas (postures) correctly.

Delhi is also home to a number of centers of **Artistic Yoga** (F-7 Lower Ground Fl., Hauz Khas Enclave, opposite Laxman Public School, tel. 11/4176-7154, www.artisticyoga.com, 7 A.M.-8 P.M. daily, first class free), a unique take on yoga that moves away from the traditional yoga practiced in India as well as the forms of yoga common in the West. Instead, they focus on dynamic postures that help people get into shape. Check the website for a full list of centers and class times.

SPECTATOR SPORTS

Cricket fans can catch a match at **Feroz Shah Kotla** (Bhadur Shah Zafar Marg, near Delhi Gate, tel. 11/2331-4535, prices vary, call ahead for details). Built in 1883, it is the home stadium of Delhi's team, the Delhi Daredevils.

The enormous **Jawaharlal Nehru Stadium** (Bhisma Pitamah Rd., Lodhi Rd., Metro: Jawaharlal Nehru Stadium, tel. 11/2436-9400, prices vary, call ahead for details) also hosts international one-day test matches and a wide range of other sports. The 2010 Commonwealth Games and the 2012 Asian Games were held here.

Polo is quite popular in India; contact the **Army Polo and Riding Club** (B Squaron 61 Cavalry, Cariappa Marg, Cantonment, tel. 11/2569-9444, www.armypoloclub.com, prices vary) if you'd like to attend a match.

SPAS

One of the newest spas in Delhi, the ultra-modern **Aman Spa** (Aman Hotel, Lodhi Rd., tel. 11/4363-3333, 9 A.M.-10 P.M. daily) is also one of the city's best, featuring sleek treatment rooms and incredibly knowledgeable staff who have to go through intensive training before working here, even if they are experienced practitioners. A session at the spa's hammam (Turkish bath, Rs. 3,500-8,000) is a perfect way to end your India visit—after relaxing in a steamy chamber, you'll be brought into a treatment room, where a therapist will expertly scrub away an entire layer of dead skin from your body, making you feel soft, rejuvenated, and incredibly clean.

The beautiful **Amatrra Spa** (50-B Diplomatic Enclave, Chanakyapuri, tel. 11/2412-2921, www.amatrraspa.com, 7 A.M.-10 P.M. daily) offers a huge range of treatments that follow the principles of ayurveda (traditional Indian medicine). The signature treatment is the ayurvedic *abhiyanga* massage (Rs. 5,500), a relaxing massage using long sweeping motions to improve circulation and overall wellness. Use of a common jetted tub, steam, and sauna area is included in the price of all treatments.

The quiet **Oasis Spa** (Grand Hotel, Nelson Mandela Marg, Vasant Vihar, tel. 11/2677-1234, 7 A.M.-10 P.M. daily, pool 7 A.M.-9 P.M. daily) is an excellent place to escape the noise and grime of New Delhi. The spa features all-natural products and offers everything from Thai massage to hot-stone therapy. The proactive manager ensures that the therapists are continually trained in new techniques and treatments. The Moroccan Spice Body Scrub (Rs. 4,500) is highly recommended—it is deeply exfoliating and leaves a Christmassy aroma on your skin. The immense pool is surrounded by lush gardens and is set far back from the main road, virtually eliminating traffic noise. Oasis is particularly popular with expats, who flock here en masse on Sunday for brunch and a swim.

Accommodations

Delhi has a wide range of accommodations options, from luxurious five-star hotels to simple guesthouses. There are a few decent places in North and Old Delhi, although most people prefer to stay in Central or South Delhi, which are more convenient for visiting the major sights. In terms of accommodations, Delhi is one of the more expensive Indian cities, although you can get some incredibly good deals in the Central Delhi backpacker enclave of Paharganj. An increasing number of bed-and-breakfasts and homestays have opened in Central and South Delhi. Most are located in residential areas and provide a more intimate way to experience the city and live like a (wealthy) local.

OLD DELHI
Rs. 1,000-3,000
Most of the accommodations options in Old Delhi are pretty grim, with the exception of **Hotel Tara Palace** (419 Esplanade Rd., Old Cycle Market, opposite Red Fort, Chandni Chowk, Metro: Chawri Bazaar or Chandni Chowk, tel. 11/2327-6465, www.tarapalace-delhi.com, Rs. 2,200-2,400 d). The entrance to the hotel is at the end of a ramshackle alley, and the furniture in the air-conditioned guest rooms looks like it belongs in a college dorm; these minor drawbacks aside, it's a great location and pretty good value for money, especially if you take into account that the kind folks at Tara Palace provide free airport transfers 24-hours daily.

NORTH DELHI
Rs. 3,000-10,000
The three-star **Broadway Hotel** (4/15A Asaf Ali Rd., Daryaganj, tel. 11/4336-3600, www.

hotelbroadwaydelhi.com, Rs. 3,000-4,000 d) has reasonably-priced guest rooms in a great location, not far from the 17th-century sights in Old Delhi and just a couple of minutes from New Delhi Railway Station. The classic wood-floor guest rooms are kept in great shape and get plenty of sunlight. It's also home to one of Delhi's most famous restaurants, Chor Bizarre.

Dating to 1903, the historic **Maidens Hotel** (7 Sham Nath Marg, Civil Lines, Metro: Civil Lines, tel. 11/2397-5464, www.maidenshotel. com, 8,500-9,500 d) exudes Old World charm and is much more reasonably priced than other hotels of its quality. The guest rooms are simple but elegant, and those on the third and fourth floors were renovated in the mid-2000s. The grounds are spacious, and the Civil Lines Metro station is only a couple of minutes away on foot.

At the back of an early-20th-century tenement, **Nina Kochhar's Homestay** (2 Sham Nath Marg, Civil Lines, Metro: Civil Lines, tel. 9811/022-326, www.delhibedbreakfast. com, Rs. 3,500 d, breakfast included) is a one-room homestay in a colorful apartment that looks a bit like a cross between an antiques store and an art gallery; the owner's son is a talented painter, and his works are displayed on the walls. Run by a former employee of the sleek Oberoi Group of Hotels, the homestay offers guests the opportunity to experience living in an Indian home of the upscale variety.

CENTRAL DELHI
Under Rs. 1,000
◀ **Hotel Relax** (4970-71 Ram Dwara Rd., Nehru Bazar, Panchkuian Rd., Paharganj, tel. 11/2356-2811, vidur109@hotmail.com, Rs. 800-1,200 d) is one of the best deals in Paharganj. This small family-run guesthouse sits over a shop selling beautiful ethnic furniture and statuettes, and much of the merchandise is featured inside the guesthouse's common areas. All the guest rooms are clean, although some are windowless—make sure to

specify if you want sunlight included in your stay. There's also a small private balcony on top where guests can take meals.

From the outside, and even from the lobby, the budget-friendly **Hotel Shelton** (5043, Main Bazaar, Paharganj, Metro: New Delhi or Ramakrishna Ashram Marg, tel. 11/2358-0673, sheltonh@redif-fmail.com, Rs. 600-1,200 d) looks a bit grubby, but the guest rooms are surprisingly well-maintained, with comfy beds ornamented with pretty cushions. All guest rooms have TVs (some even have plasma flat-screens), and some of the pricier guest rooms have rain showerheads, a blessing in a place where many showers offer nothing more than a trickle. Note that a few of the guest rooms are windowless, but these are also much quieter. Specify at the time of reservation whether you want a window.

One of Paharganj's most popular options, the humorously named **Cottage Yes Please** (1843-44 Laxmi Narayan St., Raj Guru Rd., Chuna Mandi, Paharganj, Metro: New Delhi or Ramakrishna Ashram Marg, tel. 11/2356-2100, www.cottageyesplease.com, Rs. 900-2,500 d) guesthouse offers spotless guest rooms at reasonable prices. Marble floors dominate the interiors, and guest rooms feature 1970s-style wooden accents and chintzy wall plaques featuring Egyptian deities. The lobby is prettily adorned with colored glass lanterns, and there's a tiny elevator. The larger guest rooms feature two double beds—perfect for groups and families.

Rs. 1,000-3,000
If price is your priority and you don't want to stay in Paharganj, **Hotel Alka Annexe** (M-20 Connaught Circus, Connaught Place, Metro: Rajiv Chowk, tel. 11/2341-4028, www.hotel-alka.com, Rs. 2,000-2,500 d) might be your best bet. Although it calls itself a hotel, it's really just a guesthouse, and the guest rooms are clean but really nothing special. If you can, try to get a top-floor room; these open onto a courtyard and are sunnier. Bargain hard and you can probably get a discount, or at least a free breakfast.

If Ikea did hotels, they would look something like the **Ginger Hotel Delhi** (IRCTC Rail Yatri Niwas, Bhav Bhutti Marg, New Delhi Railway Station, Metro: New Delhi, tel. 11/6663-3333, www.gingerhotels.com, Rs. 1,300-1,600 d), a comfortable and practical hotel that features self-check-in kiosks and a small gym. The McRooms here are clean, modern, and super-cheap, and it doesn't get more convenient for those with early morning trains from New Delhi Train Station, unless you don't mind squatting on the platforms.

Conveniently located right on the main bazaar, the 60-room **Hotel Hari Piorko** (4755 Main Bazaar, Paharganj, Metro: New Delhi or Ramakrishna Ashram Marg, tel. 11/2358-7999, www.hotelharipiorkodelhi.com, Rs. 1,200-1,500 d) is large enough to be called a hotel but has the homely feel of a guesthouse. The guest rooms here are clean, simple, and have a light aroma of rose water. Some of the larger guest rooms have aquariums built into their walls. The prices are a bit steeper than in some other Paharganj properties, but the service is decent and the place is well looked-after.

It's not exactly fun to stay at the **New Delhi YMCA Tourist Hostel** (Jai Singh Rd., Metro: Patel Chowk or Shivaji Stadium, tel. 11/4364-4047, www.newdelhiymca.org, Rs. 2,900-3,700 d), but it's certainly not bad either, and you'd be hard-pressed to find a central Delhi hotel with both a pool and fitness facilities at a better rate. Rates include breakfast and dinner. All guest rooms have air-conditioning, and triple-bed guest rooms are also available.

YWCA Blue Triangle Family Hostel (Ashoka Rd., Metro: Patel Chowk, tel. 11/2336-0133, www.btfhonline.com, Rs. 2,250-2,850 d) is one of the best deals in the otherwise exorbitantly priced Central Delhi hotel market. It's a bit institutional (this is the Y, after all), but the guest rooms are spacious, and the baths are modern. There is also an air-conditioned dormitory for groups of six or more. Wi-Fi is available at a modest cost (Rs. 50 per day), and breakfast is included in the room rate. Note that in order to stay here, you must purchase a one-month YWCA membership (Rs. 50) when you check in.

Rs. 3,000-10,000

There are only two guest rooms in the intimate **Amaaya BnB** (D-36 Nizamuddin East, tel. 9819/686-020, www.amaayadelhi.com, Rs. 4,300 d), which is really more of a homestay than a full-on B&B (although a hearty breakfast is included). Amaaya is in the elegant home, filled with art and books, of Ruma Devichand, a gracious and absolutely lovely textile designer. Both guest rooms are air-conditioned and have balconies.

A short walk from Humayun's Tomb, **Eleven Nizamuddin East** (11 Nizamuddin East, tel. 11/2435-1225, www.elevendelhi.com, Rs. 5,000 d) is essentially a converted bungalow, directly managed by a warm and hospitable owner. The guest rooms are tastefully decorated, well maintained, and have pretty modern baths. Allergy sufferers and parents of little ones may want to note that they have a big dog who's perfectly agreeable but doesn't like being touched.

If location and value are your primary concerns when choosing a hotel, you may want to consider **Hotel Alka** (P-16 Connaught Circus, Connaught Place, Metro: Rajiv Chowk, tel. 11/2334-4000, www.hotelalka.com, Rs. 5,500-6,000 d). Located on the outer ring of Connaught Place, this affordable hotel isn't much to look at (unless you are a huge fan of leopard murals, circa 1977) and is a bit overpriced, but its air-conditioned guest rooms are well-maintained by incredibly sweet housekeeping staff. Note that some guest rooms lack windows.

The lovely ◖**Hotel Bright** (M-85, opposite Super Bazar, Outer Circle, Connaught Place, Metro: Rajiv Chowk, tel. 11/4330-2222, www.hotelbrightdelhi.in, Rs. 5,500 d) is one of the nicest hotels of its price range in all of Delhi.

From the outside, this 10-room property doesn't look like anything special, but the interiors are surprisingly modern and well kept. Guest rooms have wooden floors and beautiful linens and feature little extras not normally found in Indian hotels of this category, such as minibars, electronic keys, and ayurvedic toiletries.

There are only three guest rooms (all with two twin beds) in the recently opened **Jor Bagh BnB** (197 Jor Bagh, Metro: Jor Bagh, tel. 9811/079-029, http://jorbaghbnb.com, Rs. 5,400 d), an intimate guesthouse on the main road of Delhi's posh Jor Bagh neighborhood, just a couple of minutes' walk from the local Metro station. This family-run B&B opened in 2010, so all the fixtures and furnishings in the guest rooms are pretty new. Long-term visitors will appreciate the discount offered for stays of a week or longer: seven nights for the price of six. There's also a washing machine, which means you won't have to worry about your clothes being beaten beyond recognition by a local washer.

It's a real treat staying in the converted family home of Shukla Nath, owner of ◖ **Luteyens Bungalow** (39 Prithviraj Rd., tel. 11/2461-1341, www.lutyensbungalow.co.in, Rs. 6,500-7,000 d). This historic bungalow was built in 1935 and sits on spacious lawns that feature an old neem tree that's home to a flock of green parrots. The bungalow opened to the public in 1967 with a single guest room; now there are 16, and the ones in the main house are the most old-fashioned. Breakfast, tea, Wi-Fi, and use of the pool are included in the rates.

One of the best budget options in town, the conveniently located **Prem Sagar Guest House** (1st Fl., P Block, near Hotel Saravana Bhavan, Connaught Circle, Connaught Place, Metro: Rajiv Chowk, tel. 11/2334-5263, www.prem-sagarguesthouse.com, Rs. 3,500-4,500 d) offers clean air-conditioned guest rooms with granite floors in a semi-outdoor hotel filled with potted plants. Breakfast is included and served on a charming covered rooftop terrace.

Rs. 10,000 and Up

The newest top-end hotel to come up in the capital, the ◖ **Aman New Delhi** (Lodhi Rd., tel. 11/4363-3333, www.amanresorts.com, Rs. 38,500-42,500 d), has already made a name for itself as the most exclusive place to stay in town. Like other Aman properties, the resort does its best to remain low-key, making it a favorite with celebrities and pretty much anyone wanting a discreet place to get away. The interiors are minimalist and a bit dark, but this isn't necessarily a bad thing in a city where the sun blazes through most of the year. All guest rooms have heated plunge pools on their balconies, and many have exceptional views of Central Delhi. The suite on the top floor, Room 802, has a direct view of Humayun's Tomb. The Aman Spa is one of the best in town.

Arguably the chicest place in town, ◖ **The Imperial** (Janpath, tel. 11/2334-1234, www.theimperialindia.com, Rs. 17,500-30,000 d) was built in 1936 and exudes vintage charm. This classic property manages to radiate opulence without ostentation. The enormous pool is one of the largest—and most beautiful—in Delhi. Guest rooms feature spacious rosewood wardrobes, comfortable beds, and marble floors, and if you're the type to judge hotel rooms by their complimentary toiletries, you'll be pleased to know that the Imperial's choice is from French perfume house Fragonard.

If you're interested in learning more about contemporary Indian art and don't have time to venture out to the city's excellent galleries, you may want to stay at the **ITC Maurya** (Diplomatic Enclave, Sardar Patel Marg, Chanakyapuri, tel. 11/2611-2233, www.itchotels.in, 13,500-16,500 d). The common areas of this massive five-star hotel feature art from some of India's best-known artists, including a large mural in the lobby by Bengali artist Sanjay Bhattacharya and a series of stained-glass pieces from India's best-known artist of our time, the late M. F. Hussain. It's also home to the world-renowned Bukhara restaurant. The guest rooms are contemporary, and it's the first hotel in India to offer "pure rooms," special guest rooms designed for allergy sufferers that feature air filters and special allergen-focused cleaning methods.

Nobody does elegance quite like the Oberoi Group, and the **Oberoi Delhi** (Dr. Zakir Hussain Marg, tel. 11/2436-3030, www. oberoihotels.com, Rs. 19,500-28,500 d) is certainly no exception. This luxurious hotel is right in the center of town, and it's easy to reach most Central and South Delhi attractions in just a few minutes (depending on traffic, of course—this is Delhi, after all). It's a bit more suited for business travelers than some of Oberoi's properties, but it still has all the charm and sophistication one would expect from one of India's top hotel groups.

In the heart of Connaught Place, the modern **Park Hotel** (15 Parliament Rd., Connaught Place, Metro: Rajiv Chowk, tel. 11/2374-3000, www.theparkhotels.com, Rs. 11,750-13,250 d) lacks some of the charm of Delhi's more classically appointed five-stars, but nevertheless it is a lovely place to retreat after a long day in Delhi. It's also slightly cheaper than the average Delhi five-star. Note that the pool is quite small, and nonguests can use it for a fee.

Popular with CEOs and visiting dignitaries, the **Taj Mahal Hotel** (1 Mansingh Rd., tel. 11/2302-6162, www.tajhotels.com, Rs. 22,000-55,000 d) is one of Delhi's most popular five-stars; locals refer to it almost exclusively as the Taj Mansingh. This 294-room property in the heart of Lutyens' Delhi features ultra-clean guest rooms. Some of the guest rooms on the higher floors have incredible views of Central Delhi, including the Rashtrapathi Bhawan (Presidential Palace). Guests staying in the Club Rooms get access to an exclusive lounge where complimentary high tea and evening cocktails are provided.

Right next to Delhi's upscale Khan Market,

Vivanta by Taj Ambassador (Sujjan Singh Park, Subramania Bharti Marg, Metro: Khan Market, tel. 11/6626-1000, www.vivantabytaj. com, Rs. 17,000 d) is a quiet choice for those looking for five-star quality without any unnecessary fanfare. Guest rooms incorporate a lovely blend of Indian textiles and modern furnishings into their design. There's also a 24-hour fitness center and an excellent spa. Unfortunately, there's no pool on-site, but guests can go for a swim at the Taj group's Taj Mahal Hotel nearby.

SOUTH DELHI
Rs. 1,000-3,000

The tiny **Urban Ashram** (D-12 Hauz Khas, tel. 11/4615-1818, www.myurbanashram.com, Rs. 2,960-3,250 d, breakfast included) has only three guest rooms, and while it's nothing special, it is excellent value for money. The guest rooms are kept clean, and there's a common dining area and small library for guests. Note that there is no signage leading to this place— the entrance is down a narrow path on the right side of the hair salon on the ground floor.

One of the best deals in South Delhi, **White House Bed and Breakfast** (A-36 Kailash Colony, Metro: Kailash Colony, tel. 11/4652-3636, whitehousebedandbreakfast@gmail. com, Rs. 2,500-3,500 d) offers six clean air-conditioned guest rooms with LCD TVs and free Wi-Fi. Breakfast is included, and there's a small kitchen that guests can use on request. The B&B is right at the edge of Kailash Colony Market, which has plenty of small supermarkets and diners; it's just a few minutes from the Metro station. Note that the cheaper guest rooms here don't have proper windows.

Rs. 3,000-10,000

Occupying a nondescript house in a quiet South Delhi neighborhood, the cozy **Amarya Haveli** (P-5 Hauz Khas Enclave, tel. 11/4175-9268, www.amaryagroup.com, Rs. 6,900 d, breakfast included) has all the amenities and grace of a major hotel but with a much more intimate ambience. Run by two Frenchmen who are both married to Indians and have lived in India for a long time, this boutique hotel has beautiful, colorful guest rooms (all with air-conditioning, of course) and a well-stocked library full of travel guides.

Amarya Villa (A-2/20 Safdarjung Enclave, tel. 11/4103-6184, www.amaryagroup. com, Rs. 4,900-8,900 d, breakfast included) is the newer of the two French-owned Amarya properties in South Delhi. The guest rooms are beautifully decorated by the wife of one of the partners, who happens to be a talented textile designer, but it's the service that really makes this place so special. Every morning the staff list local cultural events on a chalkboard and are eager to help guests determine their day's itinerary. They also loan guests local cell phones during their stay, free of charge. Unlike most hotels, you can have breakfast whenever you wake up—even if it's a jet-lagged 4 p.m.

An excellent South Delhi business choice, the **Ashtan Sarovar Portico** (C-2 Green Park Extension, Metro: Green Park, tel. 11/4683-3333, www.sarovarhotels.com, Rs. 6,000 d) opened in 2011 and has contemporary decor, professional staff, and plenty of parking. The guest rooms are a bit small, and the glass wall that divides the sleeping area from the bath may not be to everyone's liking (there is a privacy screen), but you'll be hard-pressed to find such modern accommodations in South Delhi at such a low price.

The guest rooms at the **Cabana Hotel** (R-23 Greater Kailash I, Metro: Kailash Colony, tel. 11/4074-7474, www.hotelcabana.in, Rs. 5,200 d) are on the small side, but the building is sleek and the beds are big at this modestly priced business hotel. It is also close to good shopping at Greater Kailash's M- and N-Block market and not too far from the Metro. Unfortunately, the guest rooms aren't very well ventilated, and

the smoking rooms have an unfortunate lingering stench; make sure to specify if you want a nonsmoking floor.

With its slightly crammed common area, the foreigner-owned **Colaba House** (B2-139 Safdarjung Enclave, tel. 11/4067-1773, www.colabahouse.com, Rs. 5,300-6,500 d) feels a bit like a youth hostel, but it is intimate, comfy, and well looked after. The guest rooms are a bit on the small side, and what they call suites are actually just large guest rooms, but it is in a quiet location and there's a rooftop terrace. Breakfast, tea, and coffee as well as Wi-Fi are included in the rates.

In the heart of South Delhi's upscale Defence Colony neighborhood, **Colonel's Retreat** (D-418 Defence Colony, Metro: Lajpat Nagar, tel. 9999/720-024, www.colonelsretreat.com, Rs. 4,100-4,800 d, breakfast included) offers spacious, sunny guest rooms decked out with colorful contemporary murals and beautiful furnishings. The common areas have computers, large tables, and plenty of books (and not just the discarded mass-market paperbacks that often constitute guesthouse "libraries"). Wi-Fi is complimentary.

Although **Hotel Gaiety Palace** (A-14 Kailash Colony, Metro: Kailash Colony, tel. 11/2923-2064, www.gaietypalace.com, Rs. 3,600-4,100 d) is located on a busy thoroughfare, the large air-conditioned guest rooms are clean, well-insulated, and quiet; all come with fake wood floors (with rugs), refrigerators, and coffeemakers. Some of the higher-end guest rooms are more like suites and have spacious sitting areas. Secure parking is also available.

Home@f37 (F-37, east of Kailash, Metro: Kailash Colony, tel. 11/4669-0200, www. f37.in, Rs. 3,650 d) has sunny, spacious guest rooms in a converted house just across from the Kailash Colony Metro Station. All 21 guest rooms are air-conditioned, and the furnishings are newish; some guest rooms also have desks. Breakfast, bottled water, Wi-Fi, and a daily newspaper are included in the rates.

Luxurious yet low-key, **The Manor Hotel** (77 Friends Colony West, tel. 11/4323-5151, www.themanordelhi.com, Rs. 9,000 d) is located at the very end of a long, quiet residential road flanked with beautiful mansions. There are only 15 guest rooms in this boutique garden hotel, making it easy for the friendly and attentive staff to give personal attention to guests. The guest rooms are sunny and feature sophisticated furnishings highlighted with beautiful Indian linens. The on-site restaurant, Indian Accent, serves delicious contemporary takes on classic Indian dishes.

One of the cleaner options in the string of garish low-cost hotels that flank the national highway across from the airport, the **Hotel Shanti Palace** (NH-8 Mahipalpur, near the airport, tel. 11/3061-7316, www.shantipalace.com, Rs. 5,450-6,600 d) is a good place to stay if you need to be at the airport early the next day and don't want to spend much on a hotel. The centrally air-conditioned guest rooms are kept in fairly good shape, and there's a bar and restaurant on-site. There's also a small business center, and the hotel has Wi-Fi.

Rs. 10,000 and Up

If you need a place to stay near the airport and want somewhere on the comfortable side, **Radisson Blu** (NH-8 Mahipalpur, near the airport, tel. 11/2677-9191, www.radissonblu.com, Rs. 12,500-18,000 d) is your best choice. This business hotel has modern guest rooms with rain showerheads, flat-screen TVs, and a safe you can actually fir your laptop in. Wi-Fi and airport transfers are included in the rates. The spa has a huge selection of services—perfect for relaxing between flights—and best of all, the Radisson Blu is home to the flagship branch of the delicious Great Kebab Factory.

Ever dreamed of what it would be like to live in a shopping mall? If so, you'll love the **Svelte Hotel Saket** (A-3 District Centre, Select Citywalk, Saket, tel. 11/4051-2000, www.svelte.in, Rs. 9,500-16,500 d). If an overnight stay in a mall sounds more like a nightmare, you'll be happy to know that this hotel has a private entrance, so you won't have to pass by hordes of shoppers on your way in. All of the guest rooms are actually suites designed to cater to long-term travelers; they have kitchenettes, and the staff can even fetch groceries for you. Suites range 42-102 square meters in size.

Food

Delhi has one of the best culinary scenes in the country, and you can get most types of cuisine, often at excellent prices by Western standards. Family restaurants and roadside cafés tend to be the cheapest places to eat, although they most often serve only Indian or occasionally Indo-Chinese fare. Slightly more upscale restaurants are more likely to focus on "continental" food. This often translates simply to pasta and pizza, but the term is sometimes used to mean anything that's not Indian or Chinese.

Coffee shops are increasingly popular in Delhi, and Indian chains such as Barista and Café Coffee Day, as well as foreign franchises such as Costa and Coffee Bean & Tea Leaf, serve decent espresso-based drinks. In budget restaurants, with the exception of South Indian joints, *coffee* means Nescafé, although some backpacker dives serve real coffee (advertised as "filter coffee").

OLD DELHI
Indian

One of Delhi's most famous restaurants, **Chor Bizarre** (Hotel Broadway, 4/15-A Asaf Ali Gate, near Delhi Gate, Daryaganj, tel.

11/4366-3600, www.chorbizarre.com, 7:30-10 A.M., noon-3:30 P.M., and 7-11 P.M. daily, Rs. 500) serves delicious fresh food from across the country. The decor here is vintage and the walls are decked with old photos and memorabilia; there is a huge classic car in the middle of the restaurant. Lunch and dinner have all-you-can-eat buffets, but for something really special, opt for the Kashmiri Wazwan platter (vegetarian options available), a sampler featuring the distinctive cuisine of the mountainous Kashmir region. According to a Kashmiri friend, the Wazwan is missing a couple of essential components to make it authentic, but it's still an excellent choice in this pan-Indian eatery.

If you're in Old Delhi and want a quick snack, head to the local branch of the vegetarian snack-food chain **Haldiram's** (1454/2 Chandni Chowk, Metro: Chandni Chowk, tel. 11/2883-3007, www.haldiram.com, 9 A.M.-11 P.M. daily, Rs. 80). You'll find a huge selection of Indian snacks and light eats, ranging from a cold *raj kachori* (huge crisp puffs filled with potatoes and bean sprouts, topped with sweetened yogurt, mint, and tamarind chutneys) to piping hot *chole bathura* (seasoned chickpeas served with deep-fried puff bread). There is also a huge selection of Indian sweets—try the *kaju barfi*, a super-sweet blend of cashews and sugar covered with a light dusting of edible silver foil.

Perhaps the most famous of Old Delhi's restaurants, **Karim's** (Gali Kababian, Jama Masjid, Chandni Chowk, Metro: Chandni Chowk, tel. 11/2326-9880, www.karimhoteldelhi.com, 9 A.M.-1 A.M. daily, Rs. 200) was founded in 1913 and has stayed in the same family ever since. Karim's specializes in Mughalai food (North Indian cuisine inspired by the Mughal invaders), and most of the dishes are either made from chicken or "mutton" (goat, not sheep). There's nothing much for vegetarians. The food is rich and spicy, and if you're not in the mood for something too heavy, you can always have one of the signature rolls: wraps made with chapatis and filled with meat and vegetables.

CENTRAL DELHI
Cafés and Patisseries

Chocoholics can get their fix at **Choko La** (38 Middle Lane, Khan Market, Metro: Khan Market, tel. 11/4175-7570, www.chokola.in, 8 A.M.-11 P.M. daily, Rs. 200). This incredible chocolatier makes every type of truffle you can imagine, plus a large array of hot chocolates, milk shakes, mochas, pastries, and desserts, most of which are made from chocolate, although there are a few fruity options too. There are also a few nonsweet meal items, but with this much chocolate around, do you really want to spoil your appetite with something mildly nutritious?

The absolutely charming **Latitude 28** (9 Khan Market, Metro: Khan Market, tel. 11/2462-1013, www.diva-italian.com, 11:30 A.M.-11 P.M.) is the best place for a coffee break in Khan Market. This beautifully appointed café features classic wallpaper, beautiful candelabras, fluffy cushions, and a luminous sunroom. You'll find high-quality coffees and teas; light, primarily continental dishes; and an excellent selection of desserts (the strawberry cheesecake is a must). To reach the third-floor café, you'll have to pass through luxury interior design store Good Earth, a treat in itself.

Arguably Delhi's best bakery, and certainly one of the oldest, **Wenger's** (A-16 Connaught Place, Metro: Rajiv Chowk, tel. 11/2332-4403, www.wengerspastry.com, 10:45 A.M.-7:45 P.M. daily, Rs. 70) does a better job at croissants then even the swankiest five-star joints in town. This Connaught Place institution was founded in the 1920s by an Austrian-Swiss couple and taken over by an Indian family in 1945, who manage it to this day. This historic bakery stocks nearly 200 different products, including 60-plus types of pastries. They also have some of the best chocolates in town, if not in

BHAWAN DINING

A great way to sample regional cuisine from around the country is to visit a few of Delhi's many state *bhawans*, large complexes that house the offices (and oftentimes the residences) of state representatives in the capital. These institutions are dotted around central Delhi and often have guesthouses for visiting state dignitaries and inexpensive canteens serving the specialty food of their regions.

The mother of all *bhawans*, at least in terms of popularity, is **Andhra Bhawan** (1 Ashoka Rd., tel. 11/2338-2031, 7:30-10 A.M., noon-2:45 P.M., and 7:30-10 P.M. daily), which serves cuisine from the southern state of Andhra Pradesh. Here you can order a vegetarian *thali*, or platter meal, with unlimited free refills, for under Rs. 100. Add another Rs. 50 and you'll get a meat-based side dish too.

If you're interested in Rajasthani food and don't plan to go all the way to Jaipur, the Rajasthani government's **Café Bikaneer** (Pandara Rd., India Gate, tel. 11/2338-7731, noon-11 P.M. daily) serves up fiery meals consisting of both vegetarian and meaty Rajasthani dishes.

Carnivorous types will love the meat dishes at **Nagaland House** (29 Aurangzeb Rd., tel. 11/2379-4166, 11:30 A.M.-2 P.M. and 7:30-9:30 P.M. daily). The food from this northeastern state is often boiled rather than fried and is eaten with rice rather than bread.

Near the U.S. Embassy, the **New Sikkim House** (14 Panscheel Marg, tel. 11/2611-5171, call for hours) serves delicious food that is closer to Chinese than Indian, including huge plates of steaming hot *momos* (dumplings similar to dim sum) and excellent noodle dishes. It was temporarily closed at the time of writing, so call ahead to see if it has reopened.

India, and Chiranjeet Singh, the manager who stands at the back of the store near the chocolate counter most days, will happily entice you with a free sample.

Continental

Designed to look like a 1950s-era American diner, the **All-American Diner** (India Habitat Centre, Lodhi Rd., tel. 11/4366-3333, www.habitatworld.com, 7 A.M.-midnight daily, Rs. 350) is one of the top breakfast spots in Delhi and a good place to grab a burger or nachos any time of day. The restaurant features plenty of cozy booths and a long silver-colored bar with black-and-white checkerboard trim (think the side of a New York taxicab or the band of a London police officer's hat). There are also plenty of neon lights, and the finishing touch is the huge vintage-style jukebox. And if you're asking yourself why you'd come all the way to India to eat in an American diner, here's the answer: because the food, especially the heavy breakfasts, are some of the best you'll find in the States or otherwise.

Amici (47 Middle Lane, Khan Market, Metro: Khan Market, tel. 11/4358-7191, 11 A.M.-11 P.M. daily, Rs. 450) offers some of the best—and most affordable—Italian food in town. The interior of this two-story restaurant features big picture windows and a mix of artsy and cheeky black-and-white photographs, and there's a small outdoor seating area at the back of the top floor. Amici is best known for its thin-crust pizzas and huge selection of toppings, and they also do a mean tiramisu. The *spremuta,* a mix of lemon, mint, soda, and lots of crushed demerara sugar, is delicious and incredibly hydrating. The only drawback is that Amici doesn't serve beer or wine, a shortcoming to an otherwise excellent restaurant.

The poolside **Aqua** (15 Parliament Rd., Connaught Place, Metro: Rajiv Chowk, tel. 11/2374-3000, www.theparkhotels.com, 11 A.M.-1 A.M. daily, Rs. 700) is a good place to sip incredibly overpriced cocktails. They also serve a small selection of pizza, pastas, wraps, and lots of little appetizers. The food is really good, but it's the ambience that makes this place such a hit: You can eat inside in the slick restaurant or, if it's not too hot, take over a private mini cabana (complete with a fan and a small TV) and eat by the pool. There are often semi-private parties on Sunday, usually sponsored by alcohol companies, and if you manage to talk your way in, you can use the pool for free.

Tucked away in the corner of Central Delhi's discreet Sunder Nagar Market, **Baci** (23 Sunder Nagar Market, tel. 11/4150-7446, noon-midnight daily, Rs. 600) serves up delicious traditional Italian cuisine and has an amazingly well-stocked bar. Along with pastas, pizzas, and antipasti, there is also an excellent selection of fresh seafood dishes. The place is romantic and understated but elegant, and it's popular with the younger generation of Delhi's most fabulous. DJs occasionally play on weekends.

The Big Chill Café (68-A Khan Market, Metro: Khan Market, tel. 11/4175-7588, 2-11 P.M. daily, Rs. 450) is a well-known Delhi institution popular with expats, splurging college students, and young families and is decked out from floor to ceiling with copies of vintage Hollywood posters. They serve up a delicious assortment of pizzas, pastas, and fresh salads—favorites include the vodka penne, penne drenched in a thick tomato cream sauce that supposedly includes an undetectable splash of vodka. However, the real draw here is the desserts-people come from all over town for a fix of Big Chill's famous chocolate squidgy cake or a thick Oreo milk shake.

Most people, including Australians themselves, have a hard time defining the culinary repertoire of the land down under, but the folks at **Café Oz & Bar** (52 Khan Market Khan Market, Metro: Khan Market, tel. 11/4359-7162, http://cafeozindia.com, 11 A.M.-12:30 A.M. daily, Rs. 350) seem to have an idea. Café Oz's offerings include delicious burgers, sandwiches, and a lot of pizza and risotto (not originally Australian, but whatever). There's also a good selection of beer, including an Indian version of Foster's, the quintessentially Australian beer that nobody in Australia claims to drink. The decor exudes casualness—think dark wood furnishings with exposed red-brick walls and large, colorful pop art posters of things people normally associate with Australia, such as Vegemite.

The food at **Lodi—The Garden Restaurant** (opposite Mausam Bhawan, near Gate 1, Lodhi Rd., Jor Bagh, tel. 11/2465-5054, www.sewara.com, noon-midnight daily, Rs. 500) is pretty good—try the gazpacho in the summer—but the charming atmosphere of this indoor-outdoor restaurant is what really makes it stand out. It's located on a wide plot right at the edge of the Lodi Gardens (unfortunately there's no gate connecting the two), and the spacious outdoor area is filled with large trees and lush plants, making it feel a bit like a secret garden. The interior part of the restaurant is in a two-story house-like structure, and there are great views of the garden from the upstairs veranda.

Fancy breakfast for dinner? Make a beeline to ◖ **Mrs. Kaur's Crepes and More** (66 Middle Lane, Khan Market, Metro: Khan Market, tel. 11/4352-8300, www.mrskaurs.com, 7:30 A.M.-11 P.M. daily, Rs. 275). This restaurant was opened a few years ago by Mrs. Kaur's, Central Delhi's beloved cookie maker, and serves a ton of good breakfast foods, including baked beans and Belgian waffles topped with strawberries and whipped cream. As the name implies, Mrs. Kaur's is also big on crepes—the Mediterranean savory crepe is a personal favorite.

Indian

Touted as one of Bill Clinton's favorite restaurants, ◖ **Bukhara** (ITC Maurya, Diplomatic Enclave, Sardar Patel Marg, Chanakyapuri, tel. 11/2611-2233, 12:30-2:30 P.M. and 7-11:45 P.M. daily, Rs. 1,200) specializes in North-West Frontier cuisine, from the rugged border regio between Pakistan and Afghanistan: hearty, meat-dominant dishes marinated and then cooked in a tandoor (Indian clay oven). They also have plenty of vegetarian choices, and their buttery black dal (lentils) is cooked to the perfect consistency. The restaurant is designed with earthy tones and faux-rustic low tables, and guests are expected to eat in the "traditional" manner, meaning with their hands (but they will bring you silverware if you ask).

If you want the experience of eating in one of North India's beloved *dhabas* (roadside eateries) but are afraid your tummy won't stand up to it, you can always try **Dhaba at the Claridges** (Claridges Hotel, 12 Aurangzeb Rd., tel. 11/3955-5000, 12:30-2:30 P.M. and 7:30-11:30 P.M. daily, Rs. 1,200). This upscale restaurant does its best to reproduce the feel of a *dhaba,* with bench seating, metal dinnerware, and huge vats of food. The food is of the heavy North Indian variety, but they don't make it too spicy unless you ask for it that way.

A Khan Market institution, **Khan Chacha** (50 Middle lane, Khan Market, Metro: Khan Market, tel. 11/2463-3242, noon-11 P.M. daily, Rs. 110) is the favorite choice of generations of Delhiites who come for the soft meat kebabs and wraps. It was originally nothing more than a hole-in-the-wall street vendor but recently moved into a slightly nicer but still charmingly bare-bones restaurant that has a few tables. The mutton Kakori rolls are especially popular. Make sure to ask them to go easy on the chutneys if you don't like your food too spicy.

The Connaught Place branch of **C Rajdhani** (9-A Atmaram Mansion, Scindia House, Connaught Circus, Connaught Place, Metro: Rajiv Chowk, tel. 11/4350-1200, www.rajdhani.co.in, noon-midnight daily, Rs. 300) is an excellent spot to go if you have a ravenous appetite or want to try the best of Rajasthani and Gujarati cuisine. The focus of this vegetarian restaurant is *thalis,* assorted platters featuring a wide array of breads, curries, vegetables,

salads, and sweets. *Thalis* can either be "fixed" or "limited" (meaning that you don't get free refills) or "unlimited" (meaning that the servers will keep trying to force food on you until you feel ready to explode). Rajdhani *thalis* are of the unlimited variety, and the eager waiters will be happy to douse your food in delicious and incredibly fattening ghee (clarified butter).

Delhi has plenty of good South Indian joints, but **C Saravana Bhawan** (46 Janpath, Metro: Rajiv Chowk, tel. 11/2331-6060, www.saravanabhavan.com, 7:30 A.M.-11 P.M. daily, Rs. 90) is among the few that South Indians regularly patronize. This simple cafeteria-style family restaurant serves all the classics, such as *idlis* and *dosas* as well as some dishes that are more unusual in the north, such as *idiyappam,* also called string hoppers (rice noodles served with coconut milk or rich gravy). It's also a good place to try South Indian-style coffee: sweet and milky coffee blended with chicory that tastes a lot like coffee ice cream, only much hotter.

Multicuisine

One of the nicest of Paharganj's many rooftop restaurants, the Nepali-run **Everest Kitchen** (Lord Krishna Deluxe Inn, 1171-75 Main Bazar, Paharganj, Metro: New Delhi or Ramakrishna Ashram Marg, tel. 11/2356-1456, 8:30 A.M.-11:30 P.M. daily, Rs. 100) tries to recreate the feeling of being in a garden, and there are lots of potted plants. Everest serves up a great selection of backpacker fare, from burgers to the Himalayan staple *dal baat* (dal and rice). Fresh salads washed in filtered water and real espresso are also offered.

A Paharganj classic, **Metropolis Restaurant** (1634 Main Bazaar, Paharganj, Metro: New Delhi or Ramakrishna Ashram Marg, tel. 11/2356-1782, www.metropolistravels.com, 11 A.M.-11 P.M. daily, Rs. 250) opened its doors in 1928 and has been serving an assortment of Indian and continental dishes ever since. It's nothing fancy, even by Paharganj standards, but the Western food is pretty good, and the drinks are plentiful—and served stiff. There's an indoor section that could use a remodel and a much more popular covered rooftop dining area.

Arguably the most popular spot for backpackers to congregate in Paharganj, the alfresco **Sam's Café** (Vivek Hotel, 1534-1550 Main Bazaar, Paharganj, Metro: New Delhi or Ramakrishna Ashram Marg, tel. 11/4647-0555, www.vivekhotel.com, 8 A.M.-10:30 P.M. daily, Rs. 120) is a great place to go for delicious falafels, pastas, Indian food with the spice levels tuned down, and palatable pizzas. The decor is nothing fancy, and the waiters here seem pretty indifferent for the most part, but the food is good and the beer is cheap. You can get some great views of Paharganj, and there's also a "German bakery" on the ground floor of the Vivek Hotel that's associated with the restaurant, but the pastries are on the dry side.

If you've ever fantasized about living in the good old days, you'll adore the molded ceilings and aging genteel waiters at the old-fashioned **United Coffee House** (15-E Connaught Place, Metro: Rajiv Chowk, tel. 11/2341-1697, 10 A.M.-11:30 P.M. daily). This coffee shop is actually more of a restaurant that serves a huge selection of continental grills and Indian curries as well as sandwiches, pasta, and a few Indo-Chinese concoctions. The food is OK, but the atmosphere is the main selling point, and it is a good place to grab a coffee or a pot of tea and soak in the elegant ambience.

The funky **Urban Café** (70 Khan Market, 1st Fl., tel. 9999/918-034, www.urbancafe.in, 11 A.M.-1 A.M. daily) features soft sofas, colorful pop art murals, and an outdoor area for smoking hookahs. The ambience is jovial, and the clients tend to be of the well-heeled variety. Indian and continental food, including prawns and some decent pasta dishes, are served, and the wine list is pretty good for the area. If you have a sweet tooth, you'll definitely be into this place—although the dessert menu is fairly

small, what they do serve is delicious and, unlike many places in India, not overly sweetened.

SOUTH DELHI
Cafés and Patisseries

A good spot for lunch or coffee, **Café Turtle** (N-16, 3rd Fl., N-Block Market, Greater Kailash I, Metro: Kailash Colony, tel. 11/2924-5641, www.cafeturtle.com, 9:30 A.M.-8:30 P.M. daily) has a decent selection of vegetarian sandwiches, pasta, quiches, and platters as well as delicious cakes and cookies. They also serve a huge selection of fresh juice concoctions and rich *lassis* and milk shakes. This café has a laid-back vibe, and the service is friendly and very attentive. There's also an outdoor seating area.

The low-key **Flipside Café** (7 Hauz Khas Village, Metro: Green Park, tel. 11/2651-6341, www.flipsidecafe.in, 10:30 A.M.-10 P.M. Wed.-Mon., Rs. 150) sits at the top of a narrow set of creaky stairs flanked by walls plastered with posters advertising upcoming concerts. With its red walls and chalkboard menus, this little *crêperie* has the look and feel of a college hangout, and it's a good place to loiter with a laptop and a cup of street-style Indian *chai*. There's also a small balcony (standing room only) for smokers. The specialty is crepes of both the sweet and the savory *galette* variety, but coffees, cakes, pizzas, and a rotating selection of daily specials are also served.

Part bookshop, part café, part photo gallery, and part hangout, the charming ◖ **Kunzum Travel Café** (T-49 Hauz Khas Village, Metro: Green Park, tel. 11/2651-3949, http://kunzum.com, Tues.-Sun. 11 A.M.-7:30 P.M., donation) is an ideal spot to socialize with other travel enthusiasts. There's also a wide variety of travel magazines and guidebooks on both India and other countries, and travel-themed events are held regularly. It's not a good place to get a proper meal, but they do offer coffee, tea, and biscuits. Best of all, there's no fixed price on the snacks, beverages, and Wi-Fi—instead, guests are asked to drop a donation in the donation box, depending on what they can afford.

Mocha (28-A Defence Colony, Metro: Lajpat Nagar, tel. 11/4658-8447, www.mocha.co.in, 10 A.M.-midnight daily, Rs. 250) is a leader in the Indian obsession with smoking *shisha* (flavored tobacco), and this darkly lit hookah bar-cum-coffee shop is a popular hangout for teetotal teenagers and anyone who appreciates a good cup of joe: The coffee beans are imported from all over the world. The food is so-so but the milk shakes, many of which are inspired by chocolate bars, are excellent. Now, if they could just turn the music down a bit.

Continental

One of the newest ventures by Ritu Dalmia, India's best-known chef of Italian cuisine, **Café Diva** (N-8 N-Block Market, Greater Kailash I, Metro: Kailash Colony, tel. 11/4101-1948, www.diva-italian.com, 11 A.M.-11:30 P.M. daily, Rs. 500) serves fine cuisine in a laid-back bistro-style environment. Dalmia is a hands-on restaurateur, and she may very well be at Café Diva, helping out in the kitchen, when you arrive (that's right: a celebrity chef cooking your lunch; how often does that happen?). There's a good mix of continental food, although naturally Italian dishes predominate. Don't miss the pumpkin-stuffed ravioli and the delicious Italian coffees.

If you're looking for a romantic alfresco dining experience, look no farther than **⟨ Magique** (Gate 3, Garden of the Five Senses, Saket, tel. 9717/535-544, www.magique.in, 12:30-3:30 P.M. and 7 P.M.-1 A.M. daily, Rs. 750). This beautiful garden restaurant is great for lunch or dinner, but if you have to choose, go at night when the outdoor area is lit by strings of twinkling lights. The food is just as incredible as the ambience, and they serve a good blend of East Asian and continental dishes, including some excellent seafood. The wine list is extensive and well suited to the cuisine.

As implied by the name, **Moet's Sizzler** (26 Defence Colony Market, Metro: Lajpat Nagar, tel. 11/4655-5777, www.moets.com, noon-midnight daily, Rs. 400) specializes in "sizzlers": assortments of meats or vegetables served sizzling and smoking on a hot plate, similar to fajitas only generally served without bread (although the garlic bread makes a delicious side order). Sizzlers are noisy, smoky, and very popular in India, and if you've never had one, this is the place to try this popular cooking style.

Olive (One Style Mile, Mehrauli, tel. 11/2957-4444, www.olivebarandkitchen.com, noon-midnight daily, Rs. 800) is one of South Delhi's more sophisticated options. The food is primarily Italian, and everything is delicious and of impeccable quality, especially the pizzas. The decor is rustic chic, and there's both indoor and outdoor seating; the rooftop area is good for big groups. The courtyard, with its enormous banyan tree, is especially enchanting at night when illuminated by candlelight. Note that it's not well signposted, and vehicle entry is through a nondescript gate, so you might have to ask directions once you get to Mehrauli.

Shalom (N-18 N-Block Market, Greater Kailash I, tel. 11/4163-2280, www.shalomexperience.com, noon-1 A.M. daily, Rs. 600) is one of Delhi's most established lounges, and it's a popular nightspot thanks to its well-stocked bar and regular guest appearances by top DJs and musicians. The atmosphere is chic without being overly formal, and the tables are few enough that patrons can expect a lot of personalized attention from servers. The focus is on Middle Eastern food and Mediterranean grills, and the mezze platters are the best in town. They also have an excellent wine list, and the mojitos are to die for.

One of the most popular eateries in South Delhi, the trendy **TLR** (31 Hauz Khas Village, Metro: Green Park, tel. 11/4608-0533, www.tlrcafe.com, 11 A.M.-midnight daily, Rs. 450) was instrumental in transforming Hauz Khas

Village from an arts and couture district into one of the best-known dining spots in town. TLR is especially popular among Delhi's growing number of expatriates, who come for the continental menu of pastas, sandwiches, lamb chops, fish-and-chips (a rarity in Delhi), fresh juices, and coffee. There is also a good selection of beer, wine, and spirits. If you're here in the holiday season, drop by for a traditional English Christmas dinner. TLR also hosts DJs, bands, open mike nights, and the occasional pub quiz.

East Asian

If you're tired of heavy North Indian food and want something on the lighter side, you'll appreciate the food at **Ai—The Love Hotel** (MGF Mall, 2nd Fl., District Centre, Saket, tel. 11/4065-4567, noon-midnight daily, Rs. 700). A Japanese restaurant that was originally more of a nightspot, now that its reputation as an electronic music venue has been reined in, diners are starting to realize that Ai has some of the best Japanese food in town, serving up authentic main dishes along with popular sushi and sashimi. There are often brunch specials on weekends, and the food is quite popular with Japanese expats.

Korean food in India? It might sound like a weird idea, but if you've never had Korean cuisine before, it's worth trying at **Gung, The Palace** (D-1 B Green Park, near Ashirwad Complex, Metro: Green Park, tel. 11/4608-2663, noon-3 P.M. and 6-10:15 P.M. daily, Rs. 1,000). Because Gung is in a neighborhood with a lot of vegetarians (there's a large Jain community in Green Park), it even makes meat-free dishes, and not just kimchi. Most of their food, however, is based on imported meat. Gung is very popular with Delhi's constantly growing number of Korean expats and focuses on the traditional, both in cuisine and in decor. The tables are inside screened chambers, and guests are expected to take off their shoes and sit on the floor. There is a table for those who

have trouble with low seating, though. Also, as the restaurant is both very small and very popular, reservations are a must.

Among the newest restaurants to open in Hauz Khas Village, **Yeti Tibetan Kitchen** (50A, 2nd Fl., Hauz Khas Village, Metro: Green Park, tel. 11/4067-8649, 12:30-11 P.M. daily, Rs. 250) is done up in a contemporary-rustic fashion, with exposed brick walls and lots of dark wood, adorned with strings of colorful Tibetan prayer flags. Try to get a window seat, from where you can take in spectacular views of Deer Park's crumbling monuments. Yeti specializes in cuisine from Tibet, Nepal, and Bhutan, including Tibetan classics such as *momos* (similar to dim sum) and *tingmo* (steamed Tibetan bread). Mutton, pork, and "buff" (buffalo beef) feature heavily on the menu, but there are also plenty of vegetarian options. Some of the dishes are very spicy.

Riding on the popularity of pan-Asian restaurants, **The Yum Yum Tree** (opposite Nathu Sweets, 1st Fl., New Friends Colony, tel. 11/4260-2020, www.theyumyumtree.in, 12:30-4 P.M. and 7-10:45 P.M. daily, Rs. 500) focuses primarily on dim sum and sushi, and the Chinese food is much less Indianized than in most places in Delhi. The restaurant is divided into a formal dining area and a relaxed lounge that features a sushi train and large panels on the walls covered with hundreds of tiny stickers. On Tuesday nights a special package (Rs. 777) is offered that includes all-you-can-eat sushi, all-you-can-drink cocktails, a main course, and a dessert.

Indian

Even the most voracious appetites will be stretched to their limits at the **◖ Great Kebab Factory** (Radisson Blu Hotel, NH-8 Mahipalpur, near the airport, tel. 11/2677-9191, www.thegreatkababfactory.com, noon-midnight daily, Rs. 700). You start off with flatbreads and a selection of kebabs, either vegetarian or meaty, that literally melt in your mouth (pardon the cliché, but it's true). Then they bring you more, and more. When you finally protest that you simply can't take another bite, they bring you the main course of the day, served with rice or *biryani*. That is followed with four different types of delicious desserts. You probably won't want to eat again for the next 24 hours, but when you do, you'll realize that most food pales in comparison to the incredible kebabs served at this amazing restaurant.

Specializing in home-style South Indian food, **Gunpowder** (22 Hauz Khas Village, Metro: Green Park, tel. 11/2653-5700, noon-3 P.M. and 7:30-11 P.M. daily, Rs. 200) has remained immensely popular since it opened in 2009. The restaurant is half indoors and half outdoors and overlooks the massive lake in Deer Park. The food is not too spicy, and those who want a bit more bite need only order the restaurant's namesake "gunpowder": a mix of ground spices that can be mixed in a bit of oil and added to your food to spice it up. The tamarind rice and the hot flaky Malabar *paranthas* are the most delicious ways to add a little starch to the restaurant's excellent curries.

If you've developed a hankering for some good old Mughalai food, you'll adore **Moti Mahal Deluxe** (11 Defence Colony Market, Metro: Lajpat Nagar, tel. 11/2433-0263, www.motimahalindia.com, noon-midnight daily, Rs. 350). This typically North Indian restaurant is popular with locals and focuses on rich, creamy Indian dishes, best eaten with thick tandoori naan bread smothered with butter. The decor is plain, but you'll be focusing on the rich food, which includes everything from the unusual dal (lentils) with meat to *chana chili* (spicy-hot chickpeas). They also have Indo-Chinese food, but it is best avoided. The quintessential Delhi dish—butter chicken—was invented at this restaurant (though not at this branch).

At the edge of Deer Park, **Naivedyam** (1 Hauz Khas Village, Metro: Green Park, tel.

11/2696-0426, 10 A.M.-11 P.M. daily, Rs. 140) features some of the tastiest South Indian food in town. They offer all the classics—*idlis,* masala *dosas,* curd rice—as well as a few more unusual specialties, such as *idiyappam* (rice noodles served with sweetened coconut milk). The juices are exceptionally tasty, and the coconut water is served in the coconut, roadside-style. The interior is more elegant than one would expect from such an affordable restaurant and features frescoes of scenes from India's vast repertoire of mythological tales.

Bengali food doesn't usually end up on the menus of Indian restaurants in the West, even those run by Bengalis, so if you'd like to try the regional cuisine of West Bengal, head to **Oh! Calcutta** (E-Block, International Trade Towers, Nehru Place, Metro: Nehru Place, tel. 11/3040-2415, www.speciality.com, 12:30-3:30 P.M. and 7:30-11:30 P.M. daily). This restaurant serves a huge selection of vegetarian and meat-based dishes, including plenty of high-quality seafood options; seafood plays a big role in Bengali food, not surprising given that Bengal is a coastal region.

One of South Delhi's most celebrated restaurants, **Park Balluchi** (inside Deer Park, Metro: Green Park, tel. 11/2685-9369, www.parkballuchi.com, noon-midnight daily, Rs. 350) is popular with Indian families and offers heavy Indian dishes, including kebabs, *biryanis,* and creamy curries. While the food is delicious, it's the ambience that makes this place so special. The interiors are reminiscent of a cabin in the forest, with cobbled stone walls and dark wood beams. Best of all, Park Balluchi is located in the middle of Deer Park, near the deer cages, and is surrounded by greenery.

Many people are surprised to learn that Indian cuisine goes far beyond curries, flatbreads, and rice dishes. South Indian vegetarian food, such as that served at **Sagar Ratna** (Shop 18, Defence Colony Market, Metro: Lajpat Nagar, tel. 11/2433-3658, www.

sagarratna.in, 8 A.M.-11 P.M. daily, Rs. 90), is worlds away from what is typically served in most Indian restaurants overseas. South Indian food uses elements such as lentil-rice flour and fresh coconut to make a variety of delicious treats, including the masala *dosa,* an eggless crepe stuffed with mildly spiced potatoes, and the *idlis,* round spongy cakes most often served with lentil stew. Avoid coming on Tuesday—many Hindus abstain from eating meat on this day, and Sagar Ratna seems to be many a Delhiite's vegetarian restaurant of choice.

Information and Services

TOURIST INFORMATION

Delhi Tourism (8-A DDA SCO Complex, Defence Colony, tel. 11/2461-8026, www.delhitourism.nic.in, 10 A.M.-5 P.M. Mon.-Fri.) is the city's government-run tourist board. The main office is in South Delhi and is visible from the Ring Road. This is primarily an administrative office and not worth visiting unless you're already in the area; you're better off paying a visit to the Central Reservation Office (Coffee Home I, Baba Kharak Singh Rd., tel. 11/2336-3607, 7 A.M.-9 P.M. daily), where you can also obtain information on hotels and tours.

MONEY

There's no shortage of ATMs in Delhi, and all of them accept international debit cards. Using ATMs is the easiest and cheapest way to get rupees, but if you have traveler's checks or, better, hard cash, you won't have a problem exchanging those either. Traveler's checks are accepted at some large shops, but this is becoming increasingly less common as plastic gains popularity.

Both traveler's checks and cash can be traded for Indian currency at foreign exchange bureaus, and some hotels run exchange bureaus for their guests (at five-star hotels, these are usually commission-free). Most foreign exchange bureaus are in Connaught Place, and they're usually legitimate. The internationally trusted **Thomas Cook** has bureaus around town, including one at Connaught Place (Janpath, tel. 11/2341-5848, www.thomascook.

in). **RRSB Forex** (50-68, Ground Fl., World Trade Centre, Babar Rd., Connaught Place, tel. 11/2341-2180, www.rrsbforex.com) is another reputable Connaught Place money changer. South Delhi options include **LKG Forex** (E-35, Ground Fl., Lajpat Nagar I, near Central Market Rampul, tel. 11/2981-7772, www.lkgforex.co.in), near the rowdy Lajpat Nagar Central Market, and **Princess Forex** (M-29 Greater Kailash I, tel. 9811/093-767). Always make sure to ask for a receipt.

HOSPITALS AND PHARMACIES

Delhi is filled with pharmacies, and if you need something, it's best to ask at the front desk of your hotel where the closest one is. Many pharmacies also offer delivery services.

If you need urgent medical care, there are quite a few excellent options in Delhi, including **Apollo Hospital** (Sarita Vihar, Delhi-Mathura Rd., tel. 11/2692-5858, www.apollohospdelhi.com) and **Max Hospital** (2 Press Enclave Rd., Saket, tel. 11/2651-5050, www.maxhealthcare.in). **East West Medical Centre** (28 Greater Kailash I, tel. 11/2464-1494) does not provide urgent care but has a more personalized and homely feel and very sweet staff. For heart conditions, contact **Fortis Escorts Heart Institute** (Okhla Rd., tel. 11/4713-5000, www.fortisescorts.in).

INTERNET ACCESS

All major hotels in Delhi offer Internet access via Wi-Fi for guests; in five-star hotels it can cost upward of Rs. 250 per hour. Many of the restaurants and cafés in Khan Market have free Wi-Fi for patrons, including *Amici* (47 Middle Lane, Khan Market, Metro: Khan Market, tel. 11/4358-7191, 11 A.M.-11 P.M. daily, Rs. 450) and *Mrs. Kaur's Crepes and More* (66 Middle Lane, Khan Market, Metro: Khan Market, tel. 11/4352-8300, www.mrskaurs.com, 7:30 A.M.-11 P.M. daily, Rs. 275). There are Internet cafés on every corner in Central Delhi's Paharganj—Internet access will set you back around Rs. 30 per hour. Make sure to bring your ID with you, as Internet cafés are legally required to log your personal details before you start surfing.

POSTAL SERVICES

There are post offices all around Delhi; a full list is available at www.indiapost.gov.in. The biggest post office in Central Delhi is the **New Delhi GPO** (Gole Dak Khana, Baba Kharak Singh Rd., tel. 11/2336-4111), near Connaught Place. This is the place to go with packages, which need to be wrapped in white cloth and sewn up before you ship them. There's a tailor on-site, just inside the main doors, who has plenty of white cloth for this purpose.

If you're staying in South Delhi, there's a tailor who will sew up your parcels just outside the **Hauz Khas Post Office** (Aurobindo Marg, near IIT Gate, Hauz Khas, tel. 11/2652-3059). His makeshift tailor shop is located against the outside northern wall of the post office complex.

If you don't want to deal with queues at the post office, some high-end hotels will ship parcels for their guests for a price. Most bookshops and boutiques can pack and send your purchases home for you, and they're usually pretty reliable. There are also plenty of shops in the backpacker haven of Paharganj that ship parcels on their customers' behalf for a small fee, but they aren't always reliable, and packages shipped through these services don't always reach their destinations. As the old adage goes, if you want it done right, do it yourself.

LAUNDRY

No matter where you are in Delhi, the easiest way to get laundry done is through your hotel. If you're staying in a five-star place, they'll arrange for machine-wash service or dry-cleaning and can often get your clothes back to you the same day. Guesthouses and budget hotels often outsource the work to a *dhobi* (washer man or woman), who will take your clothes down to a nearby body of water or clothes-washing area known as a *dhobi ghat* and wash your clothes there, often flogging them with sticks or rocks to get all the dirt out. This can be disastrous for finer fabrics, and the laundry detergent they use can sometimes turn whites a cornflower blue, so it's best not to hand your Sunday finest to them. There are dry cleaners of varying quality in every market in Delhi. The most reputable, **Four Seasons** (tel. 11/2681-0056, www.fourseasons.in), specializes in fine garments and delicate fabrics. They have locations around the city and have a pickup and drop-off service.

LUGGAGE STORAGE

There are 24-hour left-luggage facilities, known as "cloakrooms," in all of Delhi's train stations. Luggage storage costs start around Rs. 20 per 24-hour period. Baggage must be locked and can be stored for up to a month.

In Paharganj, **Ajay Guest House** (5084-A Main Bazar, Paharganj, tel. 11/2358-3125, www.ajayguesthouse.com) offers luggage storage at a shockingly low Rs. 5 per day per item, and they'll allow you to leave your stuff here for a year or two if you feel like it. The luggage room is open 8 A.M.-8 P.M. daily.

Getting There and Around

GETTING THERE

Air

Delhi is India's number-one point of entry, and most major carriers fly to the **Indira Gandhi International Airport** (DEL), about 16 kilometers southwest of town. The domestic terminal and the international terminal (the brand-new ultramodern Terminal 3) are far from each other, although a shuttle service operates between the two for passengers with onward journeys.

The easiest way to get to Delhi from the airport is by booking a prepaid taxi at one of the Delhi Police-operated prepaid taxi booths, inside the arrivals terminal. You'll be asked to pay in advance and will be given a slip with a number written on it, indicating which of the 20-odd clearly-numbered taxi posts to go to. A taxi shouldn't cost you more than about Rs. 400 no matter where you want to go in Delhi, and it will likely cost a bit less. A number of private radio cab operators also have booking offices at the airport, a good option if you want something with air-conditioning.

Buses also run from the airport to the Interstate Bust Terminal (ISBT) at Kashmiri Gate, although the service is crowded, slow, and generally not a good idea, especially for first-time visitors to India. You are better off with a taxi, or if you're really trying to save money, you can take the **Airport Express** (www.delhiairportexpress.com) branch of the Metro. It runs from 5:30 A.M. to just after 11 P.M. daily and costs Rs. 60-80 to reach Central Delhi.

Train

The main train stations in Delhi are the **New Delhi Railway Station** in Central Delhi near Connaught Place and Paharganj, the **Delhi Railway Station** in Old Delhi near the Red Fort, and the **Hazrat Nizamuddin Railway Station** in Central Delhi near Humayun's Tomb. Tickets sell out fast, but select trains have special "tourist quota" tickets, reserved for foreign visitors. These tickets can be purchased at the **International Tourist Bureau** (1st Fl., New Delhi Railway Station, Paharganj side, tel. 11/4262-5156, 8 A.M.-8 P.M. Mon.-Sat., 8 A.M.-2 P.M. Sun.). Make sure to bring your passport, and to prove that you obtained your rupees legally, an ATM receipt or receipt from a foreign exchange bureau is also required, although they don't usually ask for it.

Bus

You can get pretty much anywhere in India from Delhi by bus. The **Interstate Bus Terminal** (ISBT) at Kashmiri Gate in Old Delhi is where most public buses leave from. Buses to Agra (4-5 hours, Rs. 221-371) depart 6 A.M. to 7 P.M. from Sarai Kale Khan Bus Stand; the cost varies depending on the type of bus. The Rajasthan State Road Transport Corporation (RSRTC) operates a variety of bus types. Some leave from the ISBT, but most depart from Bikaner House (tel. 11/2338-3469) near India Gate in Central Delhi. Buses to Jaipur (about 5 hours, Rs. 400-730) arrive at Jaipur's Central Bus Stand (tel. 141/237-3044). Buses that arrive in Jaipur in the middle of the night drop passengers at Badi Chaupur in the old Pink City.

Taxi

Delhi is connected to Jaipur by National Highway 8 and to Agra by National Highway 2. Many people opt to take a taxi around India's Golden Triangle, and this will cost at least Rs. 11,000-12,000 for a three-night, four-day trip in a Tata Indigo or Toyota Etios sedan. This fare includes taxes, tolls, and up to around 900 kilometers of travel; additional days and kilometers will cost extra. A day trip to Agra takes four hours each way by taxi and will set

SHATABDI TRAINS TO AND FROM DELHI

You can get direct trains from Delhi to all of the destinations mentioned in this book. The fastest and most comfortable trains to Agra and Jaipur are the *Shatabdi Express* category. These are seated trains and include meal services. All cars are air-conditioned. *Janshatabdi* trains are similar in speed and layout, but meals are not served, and only certain cars have air-conditioning.

The three major Shatabdi trains that collectively cover most of the destinations in this book are the *Agra*, the *Ajmer Shatabdi Express*, and the *Kota Janshatabdi*. Their schedules:

Departure station	Arrival station	Name	Number	Departs	Arrives
New Delhi	Agra Cantt.	*Bhopal Shatabdi*	12002	6:15 A.M.	8:12 A.M.
Agra Cantt.	New Delhi	*NDLS Shatabdi*	12001	8:25 P.M.	10:30 P.M.
New Delhi	Jaipur	*Ajmer Shatabdi Express*	12015	6:05 A.M.	10:30 A.M.
Jaipur	New Delhi	*Ajmer Shatabdi Express*	12016	5:50 P.M.	10:40 P.M.
New Delhi	Alwar (for Sariska)	*Ajmer Shatabdi*	12015	6:05 A.M.	8:39 A.M.
Alwar (for Sariska)	New Delhi	*Ajmer Shatabdi*	12016	7:30 P.M.	10:40 P.M.
New Delhi	Ajmer (for Pushkar)	*Ajmer Shatabdi*	12015	6:05 A.M.	12:40 A.M.
Ajmer (for Pushkar)	New Delhi	*Ajmer Shatabdi*	12016	3:50 P.M.	10:40 P.M.
New Delhi	Haridwar (for Rishikesh)	*Dehradun Shatabdi*	12017	6:50 A.M.	11:25 P.M.
Haridwar (for Rishikesh)	New Delhi	*Dehradun Shatabdi*	12018	6:13 P.M.	10:45 P.M.
New Delhi	Dehradun (for Mussoorie)	*Dehradun Shatabdi*	12017	6:50 A.M.	12:40 P.M.
Dehradun	New Delhi (for Mussoorie)	*Dehradun Shatabdi*	12018	5 P.M.	10:45 P.M.
Hazrat Nizamuddin	Bharatpur (for Keoladeo Ghana)	*Kota Janshatabdi*	12060	1:20 P.M.	3:48 P.M.
Bharatpur (for Keoladeo Ghana)	Hazrat Nizamuddin	*Kota Janshatabdi*	12059	9:25 A.M.	12:30 P.M.
Hazrat Nizamuddin	Sawai Madhopur (for Ranthambore)	*Kota Janshatabdi*	12060	1:20 P.M.	6:02 P.M.
Sawai Madhopur (for Ranthambore)	Hazrat Nizamuddin	*Kota Janshatabdi*	12059	7:05 A.M.	12:30 P.M.

you back around Rs. 6,000-7,000, including all taxes and tolls, in a Tata Indigo sedan.

Jaipur, 5-6 hours from Delhi, is a bit far to do in one day. A two-night, three-day trip in a Tata Indigo or Toyota Etios sedan costs around Rs. 6,500-7,500, including taxes and tolls, for 600 kilometers of travel; additional kilometers cost extra. While taxis can be booked through your hotel, they will charge a high commission. It's a lot cheaper to go through a private agent. Your best bet is to contact the government-approved, family-run **Destination India Travel Centre** (78 Janpath, 1st Fl., tel. 11/2371-2345, www.indiatripmakers.com). It has its own small fleet of pristine vehicles with English-speaking drivers and is very tuned in to the needs of overseas visitors.

GETTING AROUND

There's no shortage of transportation options in Delhi, and depending on where you need to go, you have your choice of cycle rickshaws (for short distances), autorickshaws, taxis, and the Delhi Metro. There are public buses as well, but they are crowded, confusing to use, and best avoided. Delhi Tourism has launched a sightseeing bus, known as HOHO, which is quite good.

Cycle Rickshaw

In certain parts of Delhi, especially the older parts of town, cycle rickshaws (half bicycle, half cart, used to pedal passengers around) are a popular way of making short jaunts between two points when it is slightly too far to walk. They are commonly used to get to nearby Metro stations. There's no fixed rate—just ask how much ahead of time, and be generous. Pulling a cycle rickshaw is a lot harder than it looks, and the people who do this job are usually really struggling even to feed themselves.

© RAJAT DEEP RANA

Autorickshaws are a popular way to get around Delhi.

Autorickshaw

One of the cheapest and quickest ways to get around Delhi is by autorickshaw, usually shortened simply to "auto." These green-and-yellow vehicles are easy to flag down on the street in most parts of Delhi, although they'll often refuse to go to a destination that they find too out-of-the-way, usually giving the excuse that they're out of gas. It's sometimes easier to book an auto through one of Delhi Police's prepaid booths, which charge fixed rates (pay in advance at the counter). There are booths at all the major train stations and bus terminals as well as at some touristed sites, including Dilli Haat, Janpath, and the Inner Circle at Connaught Place. If you end up hailing an auto instead, note that they are expected to go by the meter, although most drivers don't like to do this, preferring to negotiate a fixed rate in advance. If you're not familiar with Delhi, they can easily take you for a ride—the city is not well signposted, and following a map while zooming around in one of these little scooters is tricky. If they do end up going by the meter, expect to pay Rs. 19 for the first two kilometers (or parts thereof) and Rs. 6.50 per additional kilometer. They also charge Rs. 7.50 per item of luggage (drivers usually try to round this up to Rs. 10, which is really too trivial to debate). It is common practice to round up the fare when you arrive at the destination, especially if you don't have change (a Rs. 46 fare will become Rs. 50). Rates are displayed in rupees and the obsolete paise (Rs. 1 = 100 paise). From 11 P.M. to 5 A.M., fares increase by 25 percent; this is called a "night charge."

Taxi

Taxis are a slightly less convenient but certainly more comfortable way to get around. You can occasionally hail a black-and-yellow public taxi from the street, but it's more common to book one at a taxi stand. There's at least one in every neighborhood—in central Delhi, these stands are often right next to major hotels. They usually try to negotiate fixed rates, but they do have meters. The official government-approved meter fare is Rs. 20 for the first kilometer and Rs. 11 for each additional kilometer (Rs. 13 per additional kilometer in the odd instance when they have air-conditioning). You can usually hire one of these taxis for a whole day, although you're more likely to end up with a plain white "private cab," like the type used for longer trips. Rates start at around Rs. 850 for eight hours and a maximum of 80 kilometers (you can pay extra for additional hours or kilometers) in a small unair-conditioned vehicle and can increase significantly if you want a large car or air-conditioning. For point-to-point travel, you can also call a radio cab. Delhi has plenty of operators; the most popular are **Meru Cabs** (tel. 11/4422-4422, www.merucabs. com), **Mega Cabs** (tel. 11/4141-4141, www. megacabs.com), and **Easy Cabs** (tel. 11/4343-4343, www.easycabs.com).

Metro

One of the fastest and easiest ways to get around town is by **Delhi Metro** (www.delhi-metrorail.com), an enormous rapid-transit system with 142 aboveground and underground stations spread around the city and surrounding suburbs. The Metro runs every day from around 6 A.M. until 11 P.M. There's a special women-only compartment at the end of each train, usually much less crowded and much more hospitable to solo female travelers.

If you don't plan to use the Metro much during your stay, you can buy single-use tokens (fares range Rs. 8-30, depending on the distance traveled). However, the lines at ticket counters can get quite long, so it's easier to purchase a Tourist Card or Travel Card. Tourist cards are valid for unlimited travel for a duration of either one (Rs. 100) or three (Rs. 250) calendar days. Travel Cards, sometimes referred to as Smart Cards, work on a per-journey basis (fare

The Delhi Metro is a convenient and inexpensive way to get around town.

is deducted for each journey). You need to put at least Rs. 50 (and up to Rs. 800) credit on your card when you get it. There's a Rs. 50 refundable deposit on both Tourist and Travel Cards.

HOHO

Delhi Tourism's **Hop On-Hop Off (HOHO)** (tel. 1800/102-9500, www.hohodelhi.com) bus is a great way to see the sights at your leisure. This air-conditioned sightseeing bus covers most of the major attractions in Delhi and runs every 30 minutes 8:45 A.M.-7:15 P.M.; tickets (Rs. 300 adults, Rs. 150 children under 90 centimeters) can be bought online or at any one of the 19 bus pick-up points around town. An English-speaking "Guest Relations Executive" sits on board all the buses and can give advice and itinerary suggestions to passengers.

Tours

Delhi Transport Corporation's **Delhi Darshan** (Delhi Darshan Counter, Scindia House,

Connaught Place, tel. 11/2884-4192, ext. 244, www.dtc.nic.in, Rs. 200 adults, Rs. 100 ages 5-12, free under age 5) tour bus leaves from Scindia House in Connaught Place every morning at 9:15 A.M. and picks up passengers at Delhi Tourism on Baba Kharak Singh Road and India Tourism on Janpath before starting the day's tour. They stop at Raj Ghat, Red Fort, the Birla Mandir, Qutb Minar, Lotus Temple, and Humayun's Tomb before dropping all passengers at the Akshardam Temple; you must then find your way home independently.

Delhi Tourism operates half-day (Rs. 200) and full-day (Rs. 300) tours of Delhi's top sights Tuesday-Sunday. Morning tours run 9 A.M.-1:30 P.M. and cover the Gandhi Smriti, Birla Mandir, Qutb Minar, and Lotus Temple. Afternoon tours run 2:15-5:45 P.M. and go to the Red Fort, Rajghat, and Humayun's Tomb. Tours can be booked from Delhi Tourism's office (Baba Kharak Singh Rd., tel. 11/2336-3607, www.delhitourism.gov.in, 7 A.M.-9 P.M. daily

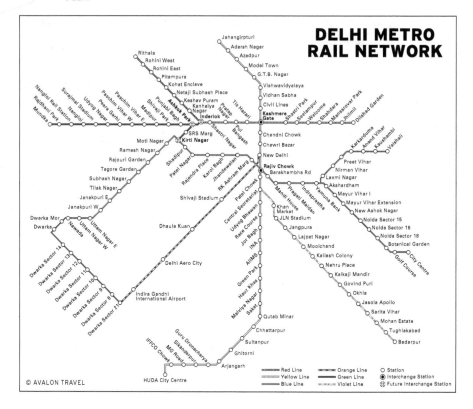

DELHI METRO RAIL NETWORK

© AVALON TRAVEL

Red Line
Yellow Line
Blue Line
Orange Line
Green Line
Violet Line
○ Station
◉ Interchange Station
⊕ Future Interchange Station

A number of private operators also provide tours in Delhi, with Old Delhi being the most popular; it's also the most walkable and one of the more historic parts of town. **When in India Tours** (R-6 South Extension II, tel. 9958/077-066, www.wheninindia.com) operates three-hour tours of Old Delhi using cycle rickshaws. These tours cost a whopping Rs. 2,560 but include informative guides, tea and water, and transportation on cycle rickshaws. Admission to monuments is extra.

The more adventurous can go on a much more reasonably priced early-morning bike tour with **Delhi by Cycle** (Siddarth Niwas

144/3, Hari Nagar Ashram, tel. 11/6464-5906, www.delhibycycle.com, Rs. 1,450). The cost of the three-hour tour includes a bicycle and optional helmet rental, guide fees, tea, water, breakfast, and snacks. Four tours that cover different parts of the city are offered.

Escape Delhi (C-192 Sarvodaya Enclave, tel. 9999/438-784, www.escapedelhi.com) offers weekend outings from Delhi, usually involving outdoor activities such as river rafting, trekking, parasailing, and even skiing. They also organize weekends of camping and music at a lakeside luxury campsite about 1.5 hours' drive from Delhi.